Men and Women

Other titles by the authors of Men and Women *published by*
Cowley Publications

Also by Ann Belford Ulanov
Picturing God
The Wisdom of the Psyche

Also by Philip Turner
Sex, Money and Power

Also by Helen Oppenheimer
The Hope of Heaven: What Happens When We Die?

Ann Belford Ulanov
Barry Ulanov
Philip Turner
Elizabeth Zarelli Turner
Victor Preller
Helen Oppenheimer

MEN AND WOMEN

Sexual Ethics in Turbulent Times

Edited by Philip Turner

1989
Cowley Publications
Cambridge, Massachusetts

Copyright © 1989 by Philip Turner

Published in the United States of America by Cowley
Publications, a division of the Society of St. John the
Evangelist. All rights reserved. No portion of this book may
be reproduced in whole or in part without the consent of
Cowley Publications except in the case of brief quotations
embodied in critical articles and reviews.

International Standard Book Number: 0-936384-72-7 paper

0-936384-75-1 cloth

Library of Congress Number: 88-37002

Library of Congress Cataloging-in-Publications Data

Men and women: sexual ethics in turbulent times / Ann Belford
Ulanov . . . [et al.] ; edited by Philip Turner.

p. cm.

Includes index.

Contents: Mapping the territory / by Philip Turner — Two
sexes / by Ann Belford Ulanov — Limited engagements / by
Philip Turner — Two shall become one / by Helen Oppenheimer
— Sexual ethics and the single life / by Victor Preller — Love,
marriage, and friendship / by Elizabeth Zarelli Turner — The
limits of permissiveness / by Barry Ulanov.

ISBN: 0-936384-72-7

1. Sex—Religious aspects—Christianity. 2. Sex role—Religious
aspects—Christianity. 3. Sex—Moral and ethical aspects. 4.
Anglican Communion—Doctrines. I. Ulanov, Ann Belford. II.
Turner, Philip, 1935 – .

BT708.M45 1989

241'.66—dc19   88-37002

Cowley Publications
980 Memorial Drive
Cambridge, MA 02138

ACKNOWLEDGMENTS

The publication of this volume calls for a word of thanks to the members of All Saints Parish, Princeton and particularly to their Rector, the Rev. Dr. Orley Swartzentruber, who provided the impetus and support necessary for the writing and editing of these essays. It was their hope that a collection like this one might help the church address in a responsible way the many issues concerning sexual ethics that now confront it, and that Christian reflections on these matters might be sufficiently comprehensive in their focus and adequately rooted in both Christian belief and human knowledge. The essays in this volume have been written with these purposes in mind and in the hope that each might contribute to their fulfillment.

CONTRIBUTORS

Philip Turner is Professor of Christian Ethics at the General Seminary in New York. His writings include *Sex, Money and Power* and *Divorce in Christian Perspective.*

Ann Belford Ulanov, Professor of Psychiatry and Religion at Union Theological Seminary in New York. Her many books include *The Feminine in Jungian Psychology and Christian Theology, Picturing God,* and *The Wisdom of the Psyche.* Ann Ulanov is also a Psychoanalyst in private practice.

Helen Oppenheimer studied philosophy at Oxford and taught at Cuddesdon Theological College. She is the author of *The Hope of Heaven, The Hope of Happiness* and *The Character of Christian Morality.*

Victor Preller, author of *Divine Science and the Science of God,* is Professor of Religion at Princeton University and Master of the Graduate College. He is a priest of the Oratory of the Good Shepherd.

Elizabeth Zarelli Turner, an Episcopal priest, is Associate to the Rector for Christian Education at St. James' Church in New York City and editor of the *Ecumenical Bulletin.*

Barry Ulanov is McIntosh Professor of English Emeritus at Barnard College. His writings include *The Two Worlds of American Art, Sources and Resources: The Literary Traditions of Christian Humanism, The Making of a Modern Saint,* and *The Prayers of St. Augustine.* He and his wife Ann Ulanov have collaborated on a number of works including *Religion and the Unconscious* and *The Witch and the Clown.*

vii

Table of Contents

MAPPING THE TERRITORY

Philip Turner

The essays that follow all concern men, women and their relationships one with another. They have been written because of the numerous changes sexual relations have undergone in the past few decades and because relations between the sexes are so unsettled: their fluid and volatile nature produces both creative and destructive forces which can leave us either confused and hurt or exhilarated and challenged. It would be misleading to say simply, as some do, that the sexes are now embattled. It would be equally misleading to say, as others do, that the changing relations between men and women portend only good. Such descriptions are one-sided in ways that ignore either the possibilities for cooperation, community and health on the one hand, or the possibilities for isolation and harm on the other.

The essential questions are, how ought we to view the changes in sexual relations and what ought we to do about them? These questions are ones faced by our entire society, but for several very good reasons they press upon the Christian churches with particular force.

The first is psychological. As Michel Foucault has reminded us, the word "sexuality" serves in our time a function similar to that of the word "soul" in a previous age.[1] Like "soul," "sexuality" is used to unite the various aspects of our identity. Our "sexuality," like our "soul," has become a metaphor for who we are.If relations between the sexes are unsettled, then souls are unsettled, and it is surely a sign of this state of affairs that the interest in "spirituality" now common in the churches is so closely related to an interest in "sexuality." The two conversations so often become one because they pursue an answer to the same question—"Who are we?" In part, the business of the churches concerns troubled souls, so the present state of volatility between men and women cannot help but affect the churches at a place very close to the center of their lives.

The second pressure upon the churches is sociological. As a social fact, religion gives expression to, and serves to strengthen, the common life of society. Like birth and death, relations between the sexes are matters to which every society must attach a meaning and for which they must provide some order. When it happens that both the meaning and the order which society provides are unsettled, religious belief and practice are unsettled as well. The meaning and order of this world will always be treated as religious matters. Society, even secular society, insists that it be so. For this reason alone, the churches cannot escape the current debate over relations between the sexes. General social pressure will not allow it. Society always demands of religion either a blessing or a curse on its own life and when the dimension of life involved is as central as relations between the sexes, the pressures for the uttering of curses and blessings will be irresistible.

The third pressure upon the churches is theological. There are reasons stemming from the most fundamental of Christian beliefs that make the present social debate unavoidably an ecclesial one as well. The very language which forms and gives expression to Christian belief, piety and experience is taken to an extraordinary degree from language used to describe the relation between men and women. The image of begetting (the Father begets the Son) is used to describe one aspect of the inner nature of God's own life. The images of love and marriage are used to describe Christ's relation with the church (they become "one flesh" or "one body") and (in that God in Christ is said to be the lover of our souls) the images of courtship, love, and sexual intercourse are used to describe God's relationship to our most inner and secret life.

Furthermore, the Spirit of God is said to make its presence known most immediately in transformed relationships between people. In particular, a transformed relation between men and women has from the beginning been thought to be a sign of and witness to the presence of God's Spirit in the church. Indeed, the transformation of this particular form of relationship is part and parcel of the very good news the Christian church believes it exists to announce.

Thus the relation between men and women is one from which some of the most basic images of Christian belief are drawn, and it is within these relations that the transformative power of faith is supposed to make itself very plainly visible. It is not surprising, therefore, to note that when the meaning and order of the relation between the sexes becomes unsettled, as it is now, some theological assessment of the situation seems mandatory. Do social changes also require some change in the way in which we speak about and to God? And what moral assessment is to be made of these changes in relations between the sexes?

Questions like these reveal pressures that are in the end theological. When these are combined with the pressures we have noted that spring from the depths of the human psyche and from the insistent claims of society upon its religious institutions, a force of considerable magnitude is generated. It is just such a force that stands behind the many questions which now surround relations between men and women and that makes their discussion so explosive.

The essays which follow are intended to introduce and facilitate a necessary, sometimes exciting and sometimes painful debate. In doing so they mark out the *moral* issues that simply cannot be avoided, and they make a statement of their own. In marking out the issues, each essay affirms in its own way the tradition of Christian teaching on relations between the sexes, but at the same time insists that, in respect to its grasp and ordering of relations between men and women, the "tradition of the church" needs both correction and amendment. All the authors insist that this tradition can neither be jettisoned, as some propose, nor reaffirmed without further comment, as others seem bent upon doing. Accordingly, they probe rather than repeat the tradition of the church. In taking this approach they are neither "conservative" nor "liberal." They neither reassert what has always been said nor run willy-nilly to condemn "the tradition" for being harsh, condemnatory, and utterly lacking in its understanding of the mysteries of human sexuality. Their basic purpose is to enhance tradition by further explication, correction or addition.

The specific subjects the essays address do not comprise an exhaustive list of topics that require attention, but they do point out those that simply cannot be ignored. The first and most fundamental is the subject of Ann Belford Ulanov's essay, "Two

Sexes." There she seeks to display the religious and moral significance of the fact that human beings are born either male or female. Karl Barth argued some time ago that Christian sexual ethics had taken a wrong turn in focusing first (and almost exclusively) upon marriage and sexual intercourse. He insisted that insofar as theology is concerned, the fundamental question is not about marriage and sexual activity but God's ordering of men and women one to another within the general life of society. No one, he insisted, can or ought to escape this ordering. The interdependence of men and women must be acknowledged in all aspects of life as essential both for corporate and individual good. His belief was that Christian ethics had first to say that in any dimension of life men and women, apart from one another, are alone and helpless.

By suggestion and invitation Ann Ulanov seeks to draw us into the complex and mysterious nature of the truth to which Karl Barth pointed. In so doing she repudiates in the name of a rich and subtle complementarity the "subordinationist" elements that crept into Barth's treatment of the nature of the relation between men and women. Indeed, her fundamental argument is that at present it is precisely the "subordination" not only of women but also of the "feminine" aspects of human nature and relationship that distorts all forms of human community. These observations make it possible for her to demonstrate in a very graphic and concrete manner the ways in which men and women are called into a complementary relation, and how they are injured when this call is ignored. If men and women refuse the complementary engagement with one another to which God calls them, or society bars them from it, they find themselves both alone and helpless in respect to

God, in respect to one another and in respect to their own most inner selves.

I believe Ann Ulanov would agree that it is a part of the work of the "feminine" aspect of the human spirit (at present so destructively submerged) to direct us to the right points of departure for the ventures of our lives, and it is accordingly fitting that her essay beckons us to the place from which we must begin if we are to articulate a sexual ethic which is comprehensive, Christianly apt, and suited to our times. Her essay makes it clear why we cannot bypass the more general religious and moral questions about men and women and rush to make more specific moral determinations about what we ought to do about providing a moral order for lovemaking. To do so would be to make a judgment and yet miss the primary point.

Christian sexual ethics must begin with a general discussion of the sort to which Ann Ulanov invites us. Nevertheless, because relations between men and women can and do become erotic, more specific issues must be addressed. Erotic relations are characterized by desire and love, drawing lovers toward physical expression of their emotions and urges. What is the *moral* character of love and desire, and under what circumstances should our emotions and urges issue in sexual intercourse?

My own essay, "Limited Engagements," seeks to address these questions. It argues that though in need of some amendment and further elucidation, the traditional teaching of the church, which holds that sexual relations ought to be limited to those between men and women who are married one to another, serves best to image God's love for us, foster healthy relations between the sexes, and form the powers of soul necessary for the fulfillment of love and desire. This teaching in its present form holds, on the one hand, that we ought to maintain a moral connection between love and desire, and, on the other, that desire and love ought to be expressed in acts of sexual intercourse only between a man and a woman who are married to one another.

There is, however, one point in particular that should be underscored if this defence of tradition is to be rightly understood. It is simply that the present debate is taking place in social circumstances where men and women face one another not as complementary beings created one for another but as atomized individuals who are essentially strangers. In our present social world, men and women define themselves more as individual possessors of rights than as members of a community who happen to be of different gender. It is consequently very difficult for them to face each other as complementary beings created for mutual aid and common life and to locate their sexual relations (or lack thereof) within this frame of reference. In circumstances like these, sexual relations, along with all others, become increasingly self-serving, tentative, and difficult. Furthermore, discussion of relations between men and women becomes again and again not a quest for understanding and mutual aid but a matter of charge and counter-charge.

The chief effect these social circumstances have upon Christian sexual ethics is that they bring into being a painful disjunction between the individualistic opinions now common in our society and the more corporate views characteristic of the Christian tradition. Our present individualism produces a sort of thinking in which it is assumed that, as long as no harm is done, sexual ethics are matters for private choice and individual right. The more communitarian Christian tradition has held, however, that sexual relations find their meaning and fulfillment within a more "objective" pattern of relationship that expresses God's will and has a moral authority that is independent of our individual choices and rights.

This tension between current social conception and practice on the one hand and tradition on the other creates what is now the central problem for a Christian sexual ethic. It is, however, difficult to avoid the conclusion that the old "mainline" churches seem to lack the confidence and courage to face the tension and in so doing give a convincing account of their own heritage. Much of the present ecclesial discussion appears to be a form of social adaptation in which the differences between the Christian tradition and the social atomism that lies behind what we now say and do about sexual relations is steadily muted. The ironic result of this ecclesial attempt at social adaptation is that the social authority of the churches is further eroded and a moral vision with Christian foundations is further eclipsed.

The pathos of Christian ethics is well illustrated in the next issue that simply must be considered, and that is the nature of marriage itself. We often talk as if our moral questions concern only sexual relations outside marriage and in so doing give the impression that the morality of marriage itself is not a problem. It is fair to say, however, that marriage is at present surrounded by doubt and confusion. The unsettled state of things between men and women has in fact forced us to ask what marriage is and what moral obligations it carries. Is it to be understood as a private arrangement between two individuals? Or are we to retain some version of the traditional notion that marriage is a public institution, the moral terms of which are independent of the particular views and choices of the people who may enter it?

These are precisely the questions Helen Oppenheimer addresses in "Two Shall Become One" and in doing so she charts a course between the "subjective" views of contemporary society and the more "objective" views of tradition. In the midst of doubt, confusion, and heated argument it is her purpose to present a convincing account of marriage as a relationship which calls for a "union" of two people. Nevertheless, the sort of "union" marriage ought to be is one in which the man and woman who enter it, though united, become even more the particular persons they are called to be.

Marriage is the most complex form of relationship open to men and women and it is not surprising that an adequate account of it will itself be complex. "Two Shall Become One" is indeed a complex account of marriage and for this reason it forms the centerpiece of this collection. The threads of argument in this volume run in and out of Helen Oppenheimer's essay rather like the pattern of a spider's web runs in and out from a center loop. Along with many other things, she touches upon the promise and the limits of the ordering of men and women one to another, upon the promises and constraints of sexual relations, upon the similarities and differences between marriage and friendship, and upon the single life.

Above all, however, she gives attention to the nature of marriage itself. To use words she herself has employed in previous writing, she gives "attention to," "minds," and "tends" the many nooks and crannies that mark the space in which wife and husband live.[2] Her basic point is that if we are to grasp adequately the sort of relation marriage ought to be, we must both be equipped with the right metaphors and analogies for understanding it, and we must avoid certain common and harmful mistakes.

The two oldest mistakes are, first, to subordinate the relation between husband and wife to the demands of procreation and the nurture of children; second, to make the personal relation between husband and wife take second place to society's need for stable families. Marriage is an institution which necessarily serves both these purposes, but neither purpose is rightly understood if the claim is made that the character of the marital relation ought to be subordinate to these more general social concerns.

It is also a mistake to claim too much for marriage. While the early church was overly suspicious of marriage, the churches of the Reformation have made more of it than is warranted. How are we to strike the right balance? Marriage needs to be put in its proper place. Because it is a form of life not open to all, we ought not to make too much of it. Nevertheless, because it is a form of relationship that is of enormous significance both for those who enter it and for society in general, we ought not to make too little of it.

The way ahead is to grasp in a more adequate way than we have previously the implications of the notion that marriage is a particular sort of "union." It is a union of "persons": one a man and one a woman. Thus a carefully defined form of "personalism" holds the key to understanding and ordering marital relations rightly, and it is to this definition that Helen Oppenheimer directs her attention and care. By calling her view "personalist," she means to say that the moral content of all forms of human relations is to be discerned by grasping the implications of what it means to be a person, and according to Helen Oppenheimer, two things are implied. People, be they men or women, are by nature both social and embodied. Neither of these facts ought to be forgotten in moral reflection upon human relationships and if kept in mind will yield a view of marriage which is neither overly individualistic nor overly spiritualized, neither overly legalistic nor overly permissive.

All people live their lives in one of two states; they are either married or single. In the early period of Christian history, the single state was more highly prized than the married, but from the Reformation on, the emphasis has been reversed. Accounts of the single life do not exactly abound, and they say little beyond the recitation of things that are not allowed, not possible, for single people. A sexual ethic suited both to present circumstances and Christian belief must do more than list prohibitions. A positive account of the single life is what we need.[3]

Victor Preller sets for himself the task of laying the foundation for such an account. He believes that the right place to begin is with an adequate grasp of the "nature" men and women share as human beings, but that an adequate grasp of human nature is exactly what we lack. The most common view is naturalistic and individualistic: human beings are creatures with a complex of psychological and biological needs and wants, and endowed with the "right" to pursue the satisfactions they desire.

On this view, both single and married life are social institutions designed to provide the satisfaction of private desires. Victor Preller is aware that there is no one conclusive argument against such a view, but he asks quesitons designed to show its inadequacy. Can the pursuit of individual gratification and pleasure provide an adequate basis for any form of common life, and can it produce the sort of character we admire and wish to emulate?

Once the hedonism of most contemporary notions of the moral life is unmasked, it is difficult to make a convincing case. Victor Preller has some hope that we might be open to a more adequate view. Human nature is more complex than psychobiology allows; the split between nature and culture upon which contemporary anthropology rests is misleading. It is more adequate to assume that society is as much a part of our nature as psychobiology, that it is our nature as men and women to live together in society and pursue a good common to us both. This common pursuit is what most distinguishes us as human beings, and what we can most reasonably refer to as our nature.

It is this anthropology that provides the signal point from which we can chart the moral shape of both the single and married state. The goods of the single life, like those of the married life, are best perceived if we understand that men and women are first of all social beings; they are intended to find their particular good by joint pursuit of a common one. If we begin at this point, two very positive results will follow.

First, we will see that the single life is neither more nor less "natural" than the married life. Each has its own particular set of goods, but neither is more in accord with human nature than the other. In the second place, we will develop a moral vocabulary with which to order and understand the sexual lives of both married and single people, one far more adequate than that of the "new reformers"—who wish to jettison traditional teaching for teaching more in accord with "contemporary science"—or the "traditionalists," for whom tradition is dogmatic references to biblical texts or ecclesial pronouncements. Victor Preller invites us to understand the single life on the same basis as we would the married life, as one way that men and women together pursue a common good.

Whether married or single, men and women are intended for the company of one another. Relations of various sorts between the sexes are necessary if this common life is to be as rich as God intends. The types of relationship possible are numerous indeed. Nevertheless, the more equal circumstances that now obtain between men and women have made one of these forms of particular moral significance. Growing equality between men and women has opened the possibility that they might become friends. An adequate sexual ethic cannot ignore the moral implications of this fact.

But given the fact that opposite-sex friendships are now part of our experience, what relation exists between erotic love, and marriage on the one hand and friendship on the other? How are these relationships similar and how are they different? And, to probe even more deeply, because of the very differences which make up their complementarity, are friendships between men and women more limited than ones between members of the same sex, or do they have significant differences in both their nature and their moral requirements?

These are the questions that claim the attention of Elizabeth Zarelli Turner in "Love, Marriage and Friendship." Changes in the relations between men and women have opened the possibility of friendship between the sexes, but we need to grasp once again the nature of friendship and the extent of its moral requirements if this welcome development is to enrich our lives rather than impoverish them. To this end, she reviews the classical and Christian traditions of friendship, and in so doing provides us with a picture of its nature and particular obligations which can easily be adapted to present circumstances.

She shows that while lovers may be friends, and married couples may be friends, lovers, and mates, it is nevertheless crucial that friendship, erotic love, and marriage not be simply run together and made one thing. Each has its own nature and its own set of obligations. Each is, in principle, compatible with the other but, because of the differences between them, they also can come into serious conflict. Our tendency to run the various forms of relationship between the sexes together into a vague amalgam of more or less similar notions (i.e. she is my friend, lover, and wife) reflects both possibilities for the enrichment of relations between men and women and for their trivialization.

It is Elizabeth Zarelli Turner's contention that enrichment depends upon making careful distinctions between the meanings and obligations we attach to the various forms of relationship possible between men and women. In this way, she joins with Helen Oppenheimer in reminding us that we have lost touch with the meaning and moral content of some of our most basic forms of relationship (friendship, erotic love and marriage) and by insisting that we cannot possibly reflect on relations between men and women in an adequate way unless we are careful about the images and metaphors we use to probe and shape their meaning and form.

The first five essays in this collection address basic points which simply must be considered if an adequate account is to be given of the moral issues involved in the relations between men and women. Nevertheless, unless discussion of these points is placed in the right context their significance will be lost and their effectiveness weakened. It is Barry Ulanov's discussion in "The Limits of Permissivenenss" that provides the necessary context for an ethic of sexual relations that both accords with Christian belief and with the conditions required for healthy relations between men and women. His fundamental argument is that we must understand relations between men and women as a divinely given permission which at one and the same time shows us the purpose of our relations and the limits of the permission we have to enter them.

God creates us in his own image to be "persons" in relation, embodied beings, men and women, with freedom and reason who have both the need and the capacity to love God and one another. In enunciating this theme, Barry Ulanov continues the personalist arguments of Helen Oppenheimer and locates them even more explicitly within the context of our life with God who is a trinity of persons with one nature.

Our society, he notes, is rightly called a "permissive" one. All forms of sexual activity are not only practiced but extolled. Permissiveness run wild exposes the dark side of human freedom and for this reason it is on occasion easy to forget that God himself is, in a very important way, permissive. He has given us freedom to love; in doing so, he has given us also the freedom to love in ways that are inadequate, wrong, and destructive. It is, therefore, God's gift of freedom that makes possible the great drama of our lives, a drama in which God himself takes hold of us, wrestles with our stubborn will, and teaches us in our very freedom to love rightly and steadfastly.

We are from head to toe sexual beings, and God's great struggle to teach us love and give us freedom does not take place apart from this very central aspect of our nature. The great temptation we face as sexual beings is to deny that what we want, in and through our relations with the opposite sex, is to know other persons in all their depth and complexity and to settle instead for appearance and contact with surfaces. Barry Ulanov defines pornography and obscenity by their focus upon surfaces, their insistence on making things appear to be what they are not. As such they symbolize, by means of their very reductions and distortions, what men and women do one to another when they are unable to love as they ought. They reduce the complexity of personhood to surfaces and misrepresent the nature of sexual relations in a way that in extreme cases can make genuine relationships impossible.

What Christians need to grasp again, and what our society needs desperately once more to learn, is that healthy relations between men and women require not only the full presence of one person to another, but also the contemplative powers of soul that make it possible for us to pass beyond surfaces and come genuinely to know one another. We cannot learn these things so necessary for our health and well being unless we understand both the purpose and limits of God's permissiveness and the destructive character of our own. We give ourselves permission to settle for appearance and to reduce others to surfaces. God, however, only gives us permission to love himself and one another in truth, in a way that images the way in which God loves us.

The moral limits of God's permissiveness, according to Barry Ulanov, are the same as those we ought to espouse even within a liberal society like our own. They derive both from God's purpose for freedom and from our nature as persons. We have not been given permission to treat God or one another as it were "on the surface." To the extent we do so, we lose our knowledge of both God and each other; our relations produce no fruit. It is Barry Ulanov's view that we are created to love both God and one another as "persons." To the extent we violate this permission by settling for appearances, we run into its limit, a limit that, when violated, diminishes us and so gives warning that God's permission is also God's limit on the permissions we can give ourselves.

It is difficult to say one thing that is true of all these essays. Nonetheless, they do fit one with another in a remarkable way and in so doing reveal minds and spirits that have been formed by a common stream of Christian tradition. This particular tradition insists that, in the guidance of conscience and the formation of character, Christians must mind two things.

In the first place, all forms of human relationship must be shaped by, and understood within, the full scope of Christian belief. In the second place, Christians ought to understand that their life in Christ, despite the centrality of the cross, does not require the renunciation of a fully human existence. Thus, relations between the sexes are both of human nature and given by God. God's purpose is their fulfillment rather than their avoidance or suppression. The complementary relation to which men and women are ordered is God-given and is not to be denied. For some, this relation will involve marriage and the sexual relation appropriate to it. For others, it will not. In either case, God's purpose is fullness of life rather than its diminishment.

The centrality of the cross reminds us, however, that death and resurrection are requisite if this fulfillment is to occur. Because this is so, the witness of the church to the truth of the cross and resurrection is essential for the fulfillment of all forms of human relationship including that between men and women. This witness lacks all power if people cannot see within the life of the church a struggle on the part of its members to bring the common life of the church and the life of its individual members into correspondence with the grace God has given. Accordingly these essays are offered in the hope that they will contribute to the formation within the church of relations between the sexes that will allow all people to see more clearly the blessing God wills to give us when he creates us in his image as either men or women.

TWO SEXES

Ann Belford Ulanov

How should Christians look at being male or female in our time? How should they confront their sexuality? What are the fundamental questions which must be addressed? What is the framework Judeo-Christian tradition provides here? There could, after all, be other ways to take up this topic. What issues emerge when we look at men, women, and sexuality in this setting, in this way? The words of the creation text of Genesis 1:27, "So God created man in his image, in the image of God created he him; male and female created he them," outline the borders of the territory to be enclosed. God makes us; God makes us as men and women both, a differentiation and relation clearly fundamental to God's creation, and as some of us understand it, the principal way we participate in the image of God. This fundamental intention of our maker, this differentiation, is underlined in the second creation narrative of Genesis 2: 18-24. There God says simply enough: it is not good for us to be alone, and so our maker creates a mate, a partner so equal and mutual that "female and male together become one flesh that is wholeness rather than isolation."[1] Sexuality thus designates a way we can experience the image of God, without either designating that God is sexual or can be defined as male or female.[2]

Sexuality is a signal point of creation, then, and not just a biological event, nor a cultural or psychological or political fact. It is also, and in the most profound way, a theological fact. Intrinsic to our relation with God, as creature to creator, exists our relation to each other as women and men, as beings who are both the same and different from each other. This theological fact means sexuality always existed as pointer and symbol of the wider, deeper relation to God. Inextricably, sexuality connects with spirituality.

This *fact* means men and women who are persons with so much in common and so many separate elements cannot be asked to wipe out the enormous differentiation of the human species into male and female. If this is so much with us, in so many ways in our personal and social lives, then it must also be with us at the center of our life of prayer, of worship, of movement toward union with our maker. If we reach Christian understanding, we come to know this fact, this being women and men, is the very nature of our being. Indeed, it is the way our complex sexual nature restores being in use, shores it up. For the love between men and women, the becoming one flesh and one bone, rescues us from the despair and brokenness of isolation into a wholeness that is beyond our own power to produce. Of that we can know nothing if we do not claim our being as male and female in all its aspects.

That is what Christian tradition provides us, the framework to which individually and together we bring the stresses and possibilities of our experiences as men and women. In the gap between our understanding of Christian tradition and our day-to-day experience we find and work out our sexual and spiritual lives, with all their own dominant and recessive currents. If we are not given, or fail to make for ourselves, an environment of tradition, we disperse our resources, we trickle away, we suffer a fundamental loss of being. We are like a motherless child, a child orphaned by its father, to whom nothing is given to be found. Everything then must be started over again, invented. If we fail to bring into conscious being our own actual experiences of putting together our identities as women or men, our experiments and discoveries, our knowledge of what feels good and works sensually and spiritually and what frustrates and wounds, then we bring nothing to the human family. We refuse to let our little rivulet of water flow into the sea of human experience, whose deep springs rise from a mysterious source to renew us all. We contribute nothing. We dry up, dissipate our strengths, sap our energies, for lack of boundaries, or never allow anything of our cardinal being to emerge into its own channel. Sexually and spiritually we live and die good little girls and boys, unevoked, unplumbed, infantile, barely having been alive. We miss the God-given grace of being and becoming our own unique person, our personal self, weaving its own way through, say, the conflict over having babies or career, or threading into place the male mid-life crises in its own particular colors or the not unrelated lives of menopause, making our way to death with no firm connection between soul and body, with personhood all but unannounced.

To lose either the spiritual tradition or the bodily experiences means failing to enter the space between them where we can do our own making of being, womanly being, manly being. Isn't that what Christian tradition says to us about being men and women? That where we are, who we are, we are sexual beings living in relation—to God, to each other, to history and society. That is how we are the same and different. We are closely related and differently arranged in attitudes and approaches to being, in physical configurations that influence but do not finally determine our perceptions and apperceptions of reality.[3] What do we say to the tradition that affirms these facts? We ask questions of it; we challenge it; we make it our own and develop it into new forms through our experiences and readings of our experiences. In the meeting of tradition and experience arise the great issues of human sexuality that command our attention.

I. Sex and Spirit

The first set of issues to confront us stems from a radical notion: not that sexuality and spirituality connect with each other (goodness knows that is hard enough); not that two disciplines of knowledge must speak to each other (again difficult enough, and notable more for its absence than its presence), but the radical idea, the radical *experience*, that sex is spirit and spirit is sex. This is what Vladimir Solovyov was getting at in saying that only the force of sexuality is strong enough to overcome our native egotism.

> There is only one force, which can from within sap egoism at the root, and effectively undermine it, namely love, and chiefly sex-love . . . . Having discerned in love the truth of another, not in the abstract, but in substance, transferring in fact the center of our existence beyond the limits of our empirical personality, we by so doing reveal and make actual our own authentic truth, and our own absolute significance, which consists just in our capacity to transcend the limits of our actual phenomenal being, in our capacity to live not only in ourselves, but also in another.[4]

Only the power of sexual desire can pull us across the borders of ego-concern toward otherness. The other addresses us, in the words of Barth, with a particular question which demands a particular response. We are called out of ourselves into relation with another; to be is to be in relation to the one who is like us and not like us, to the one who presents the otherness of being to us in human form. In a wider theological framework, this address, this call, is of the very nature of being itself and thus of our deepest relation to the one who made us.[5] Sex and spirit are what we are as men and women. That is what Berdyaev asserts in his description of the complementarity of the sexes running through all that constitutes being.[6] The way the spirit dwells in us bears the stamp of our being women and men.

This notion may seem radical, not because people are affronted by ideas of a male spirituality and a female spirituality, but because in our time, offense is so easily taken that there can be such a thing as a feminine spirit. We are willing to accept neutral signs and signifiers, or what seem to be masculine ones, but are scarcely identifiable as masculine except in their use of male pronouns. It is the feminine ones that affront, those which stamp the spirit as well as all other aspects of life so unmistakably, so much beyond the use of feminine parts of speech. To put it most graphically, there comes then to us a spirit that is vaginal, receiving and pulling us in as powerfully as a receiving sexuality. This is never marked out in our worship, never pointed to in our church year that could, after all, note the fact that the festival of saints is a celebration of men and women, real ones, alive in all their male and female parts, not proxy figures, sterile, untouched in their religious mastery by their sexuality, bits of people, incomplete, sexless people.

Recent battles over liturgy and language may seem to address this issue of the lost feminine (and masculine), but in fact they do not. The feminine spirit does not work that way. The feminine does not launch a program, nor list a curriculum, or even a recipe of do's and don'ts. The feminine has little to say about rights. That is what makes it seem, when looked at from the usually neutral or masculinist point of view, so weak, so elusive, so impractical or irrelevant. One cannot capture its essence in some sexless way and then apply it indifferently to this and to that as a universal corrective.[7] To reduce the feminine to language and a political or social program is to make the feminine masculine—or neuter. It is to try to retrieve it through the agency of masculine—or neuter—approaches and attitudes. This is not without some value. But it will disappoint if not altogether elude the soul. For success in gaining equal time and rights in language and iconography for women is simply to dress women in men's clothing. It will not bring us to the gripping power of the feminine, nor allow its dark magnetic force to penetrate us. We will lose it in the very means of reclaiming it.

In our time the feminine has become the voice crying in the wilderness. It is the lost mite, the oil that has run out. For the feminine way is not to go up into linguistic clarity but rather to descend into the felt presence of things, the depths of the unspeakable. The feminine way is not one of announcing things but of going down into them, not of conceiving ways to communicate but of sitting right down with what is. The feminine way is not even to fix what is broken but rather to experience the pain of brokenness, acknowledging its awfulness, holding on and yielding, silently if necessary, waiting, attentively alert to respond to the voices of healing, no matter how faint, that come from another source.

None of this is to say that the feminine is all powder blue and soporific sweetness as in those once all too familiar holy cards.

The feminine is combative. Look at the images the Gospel gives us of the woman who would not take no for an answer, but insisted on the crumbs from the table. Who argued with the Lord? Who else displayed such greedy, grabby desire for the healing word? Who personifies the words we still repeat before every Eucharist, "We are not worthy so much as to gather up the crumbs of thy table"? Take the woman hidden in the crowd who stole the healing touch from Jesus and then was caught! Clear theft. And what could she say in her defense? "I wanted it so much!" Would we be so fierce in our need and desire for God? Take the passionate, unnamed woman, who lavished ointment on Jesus' head, and anointed his feet with her tears and hair. These are sexual images, sweet-smelling perfume, passionate touching. This kind of all-out loving many of us hardly dare sexually, let alone in our movements toward God.

Many richly imaginative women, generations ago, saw the helpless Christ as somehow feminine and equally as redeeming the feminine. They were seized by a vision well ahead of its time.[8] For we are only now thrashing around in this battle to connect to all of our spirituality by recovering the feminine. Our great danger is that we may win the current battle and lose the war, because we do not understand that the feminine does not fight the way the masculine does.[9]

We know a good deal about the unity of sexuality and spirituality from the work of depth psychologists and those touched by that work. Sexuality, we learn from this set of sources, carries the voice of the spirit. Springing up from and diving deep into the body, sexual desire speaks in instinctive urge and compelling drive. Body is the way the unconscious exists in the world, body that itself remains unconscious, Paul

Ricoeur says.[10] Hence sexuality is not some separate part of us which in some way we possess or even have trouble with. Sexuality is not something tacked on to us or that we tack on. It is a way we put ourselves, as ourselves and no one else, into the world. Sexual fantasy speaks our emotions, both felt and inchoate, both articulated into imaginative plot lines and burgeoning upward into action to force our consciousness to pay attention. Sexuality, bringing the body and the heart and the spirit feelings with it as it does, very well expresses our affective longings for particular satisfaction and special security. Its nonrational imagery communicates "the yearnings of the soul to unite with something or someone beyond itself."[11] Our sexual imagery carries our hope not only to be accepted but cherished for who we are and all that we are. Our sexual emotions carry into action our wishes to be not only gratified ourselves but to be a source of pleasure to another, to take and give joy in a simple happiness in being.

We might go further. No sexuality works without a contemplative spiritual element. To risk really knowing and wanting to see, hear, taste, touch, feel, smell, sense this other—that comprises the great risk of sexuality. To open and let oneself be seen, tasted, touched, held, inquired into, drawn out, given over into an other—that is the great risk of sexuality. We are nowhere more vulnerable than in sexual acts. To be fully enacted, sexuality requires the deep meditative inspection and exchange of the contemplative attitude—that particular walking around the center, that specific seeing who and what is there.

A negative example of the necessity of contemplation in sexuality can be seen in its absence from pornography. There contemplation is banished. Surfaces alone suffice, as Barry

Ulanov has pointed out.[12] The "who" that is there is remodeled with air brush and tinted lighting, supporting rigging, angled shots. If the pornography is "literary," the reader, as Masud Khan tells us, is duped into a conspiracy of identification with impossible physical feats (which would in fact exhaust us at the least and could even maim us), into a depersonalization from our own bodies and alienation from our own characters, as well as the body, mind, and soul of the other person.[13]

The reverse is equally true. No spirituality works without a sexual element. When we do not know who it is we see, when we efface sex at the altar, we wipe out something fundamental to being, for our attachment to being has lost the receptivity which is central to the nature of religious experience. We forget the surprising, the astounding link between sex and spirit. At the center of both sets of mysteries are the minglings of blood and fluids, of gore and grace, of hate and love, of ecstasy and annihilation, of feeding and eating, of aggression and holding, of surrender and penetration, of dying and resurrection. Sexual love is a love with teeth in it. So is the love displayed in the Eucharist. In the minglings of bodies and souls dwells a profound mystery, a blackness at the center which no light can explain away, or as it may be described, a blazing light that blinds all the seeing that accompanies ratiocination, forcing us to find other eyes with which to see.[14]

Depth psychologists take us further. The basis of the person begins in the body. The body-ego forms the place we reside, the foundation, the house, the flesh which God adopts and becomes.[15] Persons reaching for full life live embodied lives— not detached into a mental schizoid condition, nor depersonalized, as if living in a box fitted over their heads. The body gives us parameters, as loving parents see when their infants discover that these are their toes, and this their eye, and these wiggly things their fingers. As a basis of being, embodied life spreads out, with any luck, into a sense of a shared body politic, and in worship a full body made up of believers. Spiritually such body-consciousness fulfills itself in our sense of being very members incorporate in the mystical body of Christ.

Our body displays our wounds, too. We are members of the same body as St. Paul says. We amass tension and hypertension, build them up into coronaries; we fill up with acid that makes holes in our stomachs or floods our livers with corrosive alcohol. We turn our bodies into weapons of hypochondria to bedevil family and friends. Then we can telephone one of them and when he picks up the phone and says "Hello?" our first remark can be mournful: "Not so good." But even that wounded body is taken on by the incarnating God who becomes the wounded God, with body beat, body pierced, body nailed. The basis of psychosomatic life is, at center, our God-image.

Depth psychologists expand the notion of sexuality and hence degenitalize it at the same time that they confirm the wonder of two literally coming together to be one. Sigmund Freud's genius was not only to discover, as he commented wryly, what every nursery maid knows—that children have a sexual life—but also that our sexual life is a composite, made up of stages and parts that, for better and for worse, we put together in individual ways. Freud's oral, anal, phallic, and genital stages sketch the merest outline of the territory. Along with those stopping places we find maternal introjects and paternal too, bisexual and homosexual energies, and the widest possible reach of the sexual instinct to include in its intensity impulses of tenderness and affection, urges for union with life itself. Freud tells us what our poets have known for eons, that loving intertwines with hating, that love means teeth that bite and grind us and our feelings into bits. With life and death instincts combining, love is emboldened by its opposite, aggressive hate, while at the same time it tames and soothes our aggressions so that a sexuality well enjoyed makes a concrete difference in the world's attempts to achieve peace.

We see unexpected corroboration from depth psychology for the theological fact that at the moment of creation a three-way relation is begun between God and us and our mutual engagement as women and men. Depth psychology makes clear that sexuality is not something tacked on to what is already human, but is what is human in us, what is there at the beginning and defines us. Melanie Klein's research into very little children's psychic life shows infant girls aware of their vaginas as much as boys are of their organ.[16] Growing into being persons, constructing an ego and superego, fixing in consciousness an inside and outside world through introjection and projection—all this is sexually centered. The crowded scene of an infant's interior life circles around vigorous, if not violent, body feelings and fantasies, pushing into mother and devouring all her other babies, burning her with stinging urine, squeezing her out with sphincter-muscle strength, as well as returning her love blissfully through tender mouth and gentle touch upon her fine, large, beautiful feeding breast. We construct our egos and superegos out of such primitive body-filled images. To deny this means not only leading a disembodied life with risk of severe mental illness, but also denying our life as creatures, our created state, a denial which in the Judeo-Christian vocabulary is the great turning away we call sin.

Early infant life is not all action. It has much in it of contemplation. Fantasies of love and hate, of putting out and taking
in, involving all the body feelings and all the body parts,
comprise the basis of our first meditations on an unseen but
somehow palpable existence within things, in others, in us.
Alexander Lowen, follower of Wilhelm Reich and founder of
the bioenergetic school of depth psychology, finds in the body
the basis of contemplation of the good.[17] The body is the base;
it is meaning incarnate. Any religion that cuts us off from our
body-selves must lose its force, its energy. For it is, as Klein
relentlessly reminds us, the body feelings and the fantasies
that spring from them that introduce us almost in the first days
of our infant lives to the tragic ambiguity of good and evil. We
come to see that we hate as well as love those closest to us. The
good we want and try to promote we also attack and try to
destroy. We come to see the same sad mixture in others too,
even those others who love us and want to do us good.[18] In our
first two years our aggressive sexual meditations bring us into
these great mysteries of evil and good, and inspire the astounding human urge to repair, to make amends, the work of what
our religious tradition recognizes as the grace of repentance
and restitution. Psychoanalysts' investigations of these vicis-
situdes in our early object relations corroborate the time-span
of the biblical story, in which the fall so quickly follows creation, and gives credence to the saving possibility of metanoia.

Sex, then, could not be something tacked on to our humanity
nor could spirit. They dwell at the center of our being human.
That fact presses itself upon us if, as adults, we take up or are
pushed into serious prayer life. In Augustine's words we discover that to know God is to know the self and to know the self
is to know God.[19] Teresa of Avila described this exquisitely in

her image of the soul as a castle of many concentric circles, at the center of which dwells God. At the center of human identity, for her, lives the Holy. At the end of the search for who we are is a presence that announces "I am who is, I am who is with you." Extraordinary!

The mystery of self and the divine other goes still deeper. For male and female, created in the image of the creator, also pertains within each of us individually as it does between women and men. Depth psychology spades this astounding fact from many different soils. Jung was the first to make much of it in his notion of the whole person as contrasexual. Deep in the interior confusions and clarities of a given man's psyche the feminine confronts him—in dream image, in attacking mood and inspiring hope, in compelling images of woman that impel him to certain actions and attitudes both toward females and toward life itself. The anima, says Jung, is the archetype of life, connecting man, orienting him to being as he knows it.[20] The male-female confrontation for a man does not confront him so much with specific contents as it does with glimpses of the lens through which he views life, by means of which he positions himself toward what matters. The feminine influences in his life shape the way he relates to women, all women, and all things he accepts in his culture as feminine. A man is conditioned by early object-relations, which is to say by these significant women in his life, and by these dominant images of the two sexes regnant in his historical and social context. He is who he is in no small part because of the archetypal symbols that have confronted him, those forces and pictures that point him to an unseen, transcendent world. A man interested in how he lives from and toward what matters will want to see his anima orientation, his attitude toward being and becoming, and will want to know it in its full and unmistakable sexual identity. It goes down, after all, into the very depths of his soul. One man, for example, constantly expected his women—all women—to betray him, leave him for someone better.[21] Within that painful paranoia hid his anxiety over the threat of non-being—that being itself constantly flees us, leaves us in the lurch, betrays us.

Deep within a woman lives the truth by which she lives, nothing loudly verbal or pronounced as her right, but rather something breathless and life-changing, the spirit by which she lives.[22] This animus archetype confronts her in images, behavioral and emotional patterns, and even stands blocking her in her central path. A woman trying to get conscious of her animus will discover how her image of the male and things masculine is conditioned by the significant men in her early life and by the collective cultural images of the males she has met, by the archetypal images of the masculine that constellate her life-span. Opening to and penetrating deep into the life of this spirit, she may be ushered into the wider terrain of the Spirit as it lives in her in the country of the Self, an atmosphere that acts in us like the God outside us, which summons us through our ego-world to love and obedience, to that which transcends our ego and upon which our ego depends for its life.

Contrasexuality brings with it a vision in which we learn that there is no one way to be sexual and no one way to conduct a spiritual life. Sexuality and spirituality are given to us in parts. We share the task, whether we are old or young or middle-aged, whether we are heterosexual, homosexual, or lesbian. Whether we choose celibacy, marriage, or the single state, we all must put these parts together, must improvise genuine personal identities out of the conditionings of early object relations, of culture and archetype, of the images that arise clearly in consciousness or less securely from the unconscious. Perfection is not the goal. Wholeness is.

Freud also saw what he thought of as the bisexuality of the psyche, as he traced the highly varied and complex possibilities of individual realization of the oedipal complex, that pivotal drama so central, in his formulation, to psychic life.[23] Identifying with the mother and taking the father as the sexual object, or both in varying proportions, are the multiple choices for every little girl and boy. The drama persists in all of us, if not necessarily in the precise terms that Freud used.

How we resolve these identifications and settle these object choices unconsciously shapes the options of our adult sexual life. But more, this putting together of our sexual dramatis personae helps shape our spiritual picture of the world, defines how the great forces in that world go together for us—Mother and Father and all they symbolize, idiosyncratically, socially. From this picture, we construct the body parts of self and other, find in them our conflicting attractions and energies. The denouement of the drama, the oedipal resolution, creates a metaphysical structure for us, not just a psychological one, of the world as a whole and what our place is in it.

Klein took this drama farther back into pre-oedipal life, before the third-year to sixth-year period upon which Freud concentrated. She found that in our earliest beginnings we all pass through a feminine position and a masculine one, replete with passions, identifications, griefs, and assaulting aggressions.[24] The relative strengths and heartaches of these positions go toward building up not only our sexual identities but our body-based spiritual hopes about being itself, about what life offers, about what has central importance and how we can receive it or can lay our hands on it.

D. W. Winnicott talked about what he called the male and female elements of being which reside in each of us and which we exchange with others.[25] He went so far in his exploration of the importance of the sexual elements of being as to say that the lust for war and for dictatorship spring from a strong unrecognized fear of women, for after all it is from women that being springs, it is women upon whom we are utterly dependent at the beginning of life, it is women without whom we are not merely vulnerable, but helpless. Failing to acknowledge our debt to women, we choose all sorts of substitute loyalties instead. Winnicott says that often enough we unconsciously choose a dictator who commands our devotion as well as our votes when we avoid facing how much we owe the woman who was our mother. The really overpowering dictator is still less powerful in our mind's eye than the woman upon whom we were once utterly, totally dependent. When we cannot bring this woman's influence—and what Winnicott calls the female element of being that she initiated in us—into conscious relation with our male element of being, then it is that we fail to achieve health. For what health means is carrying conflict within ourselves rather than splitting ourselves up into disparate parts and projecting them onto others.

Not only then must we wrestle with the conflict of the male and female elements within ourselves, but also with the struggle of love versus hate, of being versus doing. When we feel we cannot suffer such conflicts within ourselves, war becomes attractive to us. Such social turmoil relieves us of the arduous task of trying to push the different parts of ourselves together into some workable whole. If, on the other hand, we do acknowledge our debt to women, the result is not a kind of aimless praise for the female sex, but rather a lessening of our fear of being dependent, vulnerable, helpless. These feelings no longer menace us, consciously or unconsciously. We feel able to carry these feelings. We will to do so and now we feel gratitude to the women who once carried us.[26]

Religious tradition knows much about these strong sexual elements of being, about male and female and about their intertwinings. The mystics make that clear in their use of sexual language to convey their experience of the divine, now as a breast, now as a penetrating love, as a capacious mother who holds us in being, as a faithful father who calls us to a new life. But the church that lives out this tradition too often shies away from the frank link of sex and spirit. We want to say that sex does not count in spiritual matters, or that spirit does not inform our sexual experience. Especially does the church eschew the vulnerability the link of sex and spirit exposes. We turn away in fear, sometimes in disgust. It does not do us credit.

II. Sex, Spirit, Sin

Looked at from the perspective of the centrality of sexuality in our spiritual lives, sin exposes itself to us in some remarkably specific forms. Always, we demand formulas, typologies. If we accept the linking of sex and spirit, then we want it all packaged in plain brown envelopes guaranteed to keep us safe from all the fires, sexual *and* spiritual. We want simple definitions of what it is to be male or female. We want foolproof prayer methods, safely demarcated stages of spiritual development and religious faith. Then we can lose ourselves in the busy work of figuring out which stage we are at, and in great rich orgies of guilt as we recognize that in the world of stages we should have progressed much further by now. If that is not enough we can occupy ourselves in contemplation of the ways and means of shifting from stage to stage, looking lingeringly at changes in world views, at variations in self-esteem, at our attitudes towards others and others toward us, concocting questions to ask others in a kind of parody of psychotherapy or spiritual direction and devising answers that will assure standing, continuity, and power for us, even in moments of desolation and failure.

What has any of this to do with the Body who comes, knocking at our door in the dead of night, frightening us out of our wits, thrilling us at the center of our being? What has this to do with the God who says, Choose me, passion, crucifixion, resurrection and all? What has this to do with a God who can send us in to do battle, proclaiming a transcendental sovereignty that few want to acknowledge? With a God who will seek us and find us, moping under a gourd, shivering with anxiety, suffering the horrors of boils, dying of depression? The God who will somehow make us pregnant? What is to guarantee our safety in all these large showings of the divine in our midst? What is there to assure us that we have not lost our senses, gone mad?

The life of sex and spirit joined together does not offer safety, but rather a certainty of presence, of open, if turbulent, relation to God, and to any other who addresses us. That is what we turn away from when we seek firm, tight little formulas that induce dizzying superego pressures and obsessional preoccupations with developmental stages.

The "right" methods to pray and the "right" definitions of male and female violate the vulnerability which defines the terrain of sex and spirit and which they insist on opening in us.

There is no living participation in God's image, no relationship to the male and female, in those tidy categories of "real" femininity or masculinity. Like Cinderella's sisters, those tidinesses perform mutilations of our complex being, hacking off a toe here, shaving a heel there to enable us to shoehorn our way into the magic slipper of fixed categories, leaving us violated, more incomplete than ever, far from the well-ordered vision we have of ourselves, and an immeasurable distance from a living spirit or sexuality.

Religious tradition can be used or misused here. We only too quickly can turn away from our actual experiences of God, alive with ancient symbols of sexual and spiritual experience and understanding. We do so when we expect church authorities to direct our most intimate contacts with body and self and other and God. We allow rules and regulations to enter our bathrooms, to occupy a place in our beds. We look at the rule book while we are talking to God. We must do it right. We must be safe. Or we insist on doing it wrong and defying those same authorities. Either way, the formulaic approach holds sway. At either extreme, we reject the gift of sexuality, with its astonishing surprises, as we discover where pleasure is to be found, where attraction will ignite, as we learn that nothing of sex or spirit is exactly the same from time to time. If we look for rules, either to keep or to break, we lose the mixing powers of fantasy, of reality, the endless range of possibility of the one for whom we risk all, open all, move past all that is merely reasonable. We turn away, in the rule book, from liquid pulsating responses, from luminous skin, from urges to pour out all and drink in all as if all we were, in all of our being, were somehow porous to being. We turn away, of all things, from a deep interior humming of being in our bodies to a sex manual about positions and procedures, or a spiritual machinery about affects and effects. In such a general condition of things, it is an amazing grace that anyone can know anything of sexual or spiritual pleasure at all.

There is another sort of turning away from both sex and the spirit that at first seems the exact opposite of the one just described but is in fact its mirror version. In the one, we renounce experience for tradition. Here, in the other, we renounce tradition for experience. We turn away from the linking of sex and spirit, simply denying that the connection even exists. Sex, pulled loose from its moorings in relation to the mystery of God and the other, becomes now not the secret wrapped in a plain brown envelope, but one wrapped in plastic. We see through it right away—no mystery at all. Sex and the spirit are problems to be solved: sex as health food, sex as band-aid, sex as high performance on an achievement list.

The issue once again is posed all the wrong ways. Sex is yanked free from spirit. In our new freedom we are quickly captured by the culture of which we are a part, caught up in it completely, and forget the theological fact. Atomized, we become economic and social units in which women inevitably are given inferior places. No longer do we see ourselves as persons created and held in relation with each other, addressing each other. We no longer hear the claims of relationship, no longer feel the obligation to receive and act upon the invading graces of relationship. Sex is now something we have or do not have, something we can take up or put down. We forget the significant words of St. Paul, that we serve God in a married or a single state, and forget too that in that order of precedence serving God comes first. It does not matter whether we do it this way or that, in one state or the other. That is the spiritual point of marriage and also of the single life. Marriage is not primarily a social unit or a social institution. It is a mingling of two who become one and yet remain two, an ineffable and all but inarticulate mixing of soul and soul, matter and matter, around what matters, being together. That is what can make marriage so destructive, a crucifixion, because a hostile partner can put his or her finger right on the place the other is vulnerable and do terrible damage. We deny this spiritual purpose of marriage, just as we deny its sexual dimension when we reduce sexual life either to procreation or to a kind of fiber-packed diet, something we "do for our health." The proof is in the product then, not in the loving, not in the indwelling each in the other, not in the calling out each of the other, not in daring the risk of otherness every day, every single day.

St. Paul's point is that male and female run throughout life, whether in the married state or the single. How are we women, how are we men, in relation to God? That is the question put to us, and it is to put to all of us, in our celibate life, in our sexual life, in our friendships, in our relationships at work, in our social life, in our communities. Sin in this setting is not just our lust for foolproof formulas and simple fixed categories, but also our carelessness about the great sprawling claims of our sexual-spiritual nature. We know too well an unwillingness to accept our sexual-spiritual reality, really to see what kind of women and men we might be in relation to everyone else and in relation to God. We lose too easily the embodied basis of creation and the chance for a spirituality that goes all the way down into us.

Whatever our sexuality, however we live it, the refusal to acknowledge that we know ourselves as this kind of man or woman with this particular configuration of parts keeps us from intimacy with God or anyone else. For example, a homosexual said of himself he was more female than male with men, and more male with women. In seeking intimacy with another man, he faced an issue in himself of finding and making enough space for his male part. Otherwise he would slide out, discarding an essential element of his being, leaving him half the person he was, impossibly wasteful and wasted. Another man discovered through dream images, as well as turbulent affairs with women, that part of his anima seemed psychotic to him. So crazy and opposed to a world of common sense did she seem, that he had to face the issue of how to include her whom he feared without being taken over by her. A woman in analysis came upon a piece of her feminine self unlike anything she had been trained to accept as feminine. Here was a powerful witch-like force consumed with appetites for all the family jewels, all the best food, all the high placement and position and force that sounded the depths in her of isolated vulnerability and tooth-gnashing rage. How to house this large female part? How to actually make room for "her" in her daily life? A nun determined to be honest with herself said she was not interested in living her celibate life only for a while, just until something better came along. She wanted to live out of all of herself, out of a "deep place" in herself, including her sexuality, or it was simply not worth it, none of it.

Those are the kinds of issues facing each of us if we take the being offered to us in such plenitude, the spiritual and sexual being, the whole. For each of us to struggle with these issues, rather than to solve them once and for all, opens up the bottom layers of spirit in which the God-coming-to-us incarnates. Refusal to acknowledge our male-female, female-male natures delivers us into a groundless place where we get no foothold and find no way to care about the parts given us or our neighbor.

Similarly in worship, private or corporate, we do not land on the ground God has provided for us if we refuse to admit we are woman or man, that our being depends upon it. We fly away in denial into an airy, puffy spirituality, where we all talk in low voices about "having" a spiritual life or "doing" spiritual exercises. Spirit is instinct in the flesh. We do not create it or do it or have it. It is. We discover it, as prayer experience, at once so shocking and relieving, shows us. All along, through all our fumbled and mumbled efforts, it is God's spirit that has moved us to pray, that prays in us and through us from the beginning.

Knowing that, we enter the dark unknowing place, the cloud of loving. Knowing that, we grasp finally that the spiritual life is life running through us, living itself, in the space we make for it. Spiritual life is neither having nor doing something. It is returning home, where we are awaited. It is being found out on the hillside, alone and lost and brought back to the sheepfold. It is the door opening, the feast prepared and ready. What took you so long, God asks. Spiritual life is really not our choice, yet it begins with our willingness to receive all that has been given us and not turn away.

III. Sex, Spirit, and the New

A crucial task follows from our creation in relation to each other as women and men, one that is our principal way of participating in God's life in us. It is the recovery of the feminine. Our century is marked by this task and will continue to be until its end. With the task comes the recognition that one of the major effects of the Fall is the wrenching of sexual polarity into polarization. When the feminine is not seen and valued, the masculine also goes askew. One without the other means the loss of both.[27]

None of this is new to a sensitive person. Sufferings, too numerous to list, follow upon the undervaluing of the feminine in ourselves, in our culture, in our world. What is new is our perception of the defenselessness of the feminine against such discrimination, even against efforts of rectification. This is not because the feminine mode of being is powerless but because of its radical difference from other modes. That difference feels so large to us today that it spells a dreadful otherness, something we usually try to avoid or, even if interested, find too hard to grasp. Even its ways of presentation differ from our usual ones. We cannot set out a case with a tidy set of points that add up to a conclusive argument for what the feminine is and how it ought to be accepted and honored. Its way of communicating does not work like that.

For one thing, it is often wordless, even mute, non-discursive.[28] For another, we cannot list lots of examples and then abstract general characteristics from them that describe the essence of the feminine that we can now apply to all situations. It eludes that sort of summary and reduction, always showing up in one sort of instance in one characteristic way and in another in its defined ways. It refuses to gel into solid, trustworthy, repeatable forms.[29] Thus in board meetings of institutions, for example, the feminine concerns itself with the spirit of meeting, indeed with the spirit of how a whole institution is oriented toward reality, toward what it is being and doing in the world. From that level of ground, people caught by the feminine will ask difficult questions or make what seem like contentious but not quite clear suggestions for action. Usually, such departure-points are felt by the majority as too ephemeral, too intangible, too thorny to be of much use in making hard specific decisions for acts. But wrong departure-points, even for right or necessary actions, never change anything. They are still ungrounded actions, or they stand on one foot alone and hence must be unstable. Such actions result only in moving things around in place without making any real difference.

The feminine mode of being shows up in various instances that always differ from each other. Hence, we must always look at each particular example in its own right and in its own terms, accepting and honoring what is. That attitude does not breed a sentimental permissiveness; rather, it springs from a kind of ruthlessly lucid perception of what is not there. But it also goes to what is there, what is immediate and present, and eschews high views of "ought" and "should."

An example illustrates this elusive but durable mode of being. It is taken from an episode in group therapy. A woman started right at the opening of her group hour to report a series of significant changes in her intense work schedule and family life. Gradually she fell not exactly silent, but still. Her body, caught in this mode of speaking, became utterly quiet, almost as if she were holding her breath in expectation of something. The group members waited, listened to this stillness, interrupted only once or twice by a few words. People had different experiences of her state of being. She was in it so thoroughly that she induced a similar state in others. So the speaking of her mood, if we can call it that, was done through her for all the rest of the group as well as for herself. Everyone spoke out of his or her stillness of being engendered by this experience. Each one described the experience differently.

The first, the initiating woman, said she felt utterly quiet, held at a still point, needing no words, no purposes, no projects or lines of development, suspended as if in a womb, held in being rather than doing. Another woman felt restless, even though sympathetic. She called the mood passive and infantile, and tried to stir the initiating woman to action or reaction. Was her state of mind compensatory for the frantic schedule she had been keeping? A third woman felt calmed, as if her anxiety were all drained out of her; she had met her own ground. Images of being arose in her, pleasant images but not resolving ones that explained the mood. She felt restored to a state she had known in herself some days before but had not been able to return to and reconnect with. A fourth woman had images of a plumb-line swaying, then slowing down and becoming still, pointing the true axis both downward and upward. Another image also came, one of sitting with the first woman in a garden swing, just rocking gently back and forth, being together, saying nothing. A man felt perplexed as to where the first woman was, and wanted more information.

All these reactions helped the first woman to say more about her experience. It was mixed. Would this stillness take her over, dissolve her words and dilute her perceptions, so she would just disappear and never come back to the world? That frightened her. Yet she felt this still place was restful, dark, poised. To her surprise, she realized this state of mind had to be shared. Being in it was not enough. Being there had to be shared and that was what had started her speaking in the first place. That was reassuring. It checked her fear of disappearing, as under the still surface of a pond. Something in the stillness itself wanted to speak out to others. But we never would have heard it if we could not have waited. And we never could have waited if we had been busy with psychological formulas and explanations about compensation or passivity or rejection. We never could have put aside those theories if we had not been willing to open to our own level of experience, to know the same reality she did. Her speaking turned out to be everyone in the room speaking, each from his or her own point of view. The spirit arose from this shared point of view.

We must all, men as well as women, ask ourselves, can we open ourselves to such a presence of the feminine? Can we wait and allow ourselves to be so moved, to be engendered anew from such a starting place, recognizing all the time that this is but one instance, a precious one but not the only one, of a whole mode of being and becoming?

Really to acknowledge that we are sexual and spiritual beings held in relation to God's inner life of relation is to live open-ended to different axes of being, not only within ourselves but also in relation to others. We must accept as fact that we are not and cannot become complete in ourselves. We depend upon and wait upon what others ask us and answer to us. The other sex is always, invariably, out there, addressing us—whether in the intimacies of marriage or the collegiality of co-workers or any other meeting ground. If we accept the spiritual-sexual nature of our being, which means accepting our maleness and femaleness, then when we are in touch with one we are inevitably in touch with and in relation to the other. Otherness exists right there alongside us, in the subway, in the next car on the highway, in the house across the way, at the desk near ours at work or at school, ahead of us in the line at the grocery store, in the next pew, and right there in our own dreams and passing moods and thoughts. In our actual sexual experience we are most at risk, most vulnerable to one another and most open.

And so there it is that we can be most deeply harmed and damaged. Our spirit can be wounded, even maimed permanently by sexual mistreatment, but it can also be quickened by sexual joy. The giving and receiving of sexual pleasure bring deep solace to body and soul. Greeting and being greeted with love as a whole person can restore hope in the enterprise of being human. The laughter and joy of intimacy and all its quiet kindness, expressed in touching and holding, can smooth out irritations and soften fears. The expressions of *thanatos* and the expressions of *eros* join together. The pull of inertia into the undertow of hate, rage, and despair is matched by the sturdy yet buoyant surges of attraction, desire, and impulse toward union. Together they bring confidence and excitement about living in touch not only with the other person but with all that matters. We must be tough-minded about this. The other faces me with questions, questions about life at its core. I cannot evade them any more than I can flee my own sexuality, which is, want it or not, ready or not, open to the opposite sex.

What is new about this now in the late twentieth century is that it is known to more and more people, conscious in more and more of us. Put psychologically, we can say we live on the threshold of comprehending in the ordinariness of our own personalities the idea that the whole person is the contrasexual person. That means that each of us, separately and together, shares the task of improvising a particular personal identity out of our given parts. This task falls to every one of us, old or young, coupled or single, lesbian, heterosexual, homosexual, or celibate. We join each other across the usual dividing lines because we share the same task. This perception brings greater freedom in our actions and reactions to each other and great progress toward making our world hospitable. We may move out from under compulsions to enforce the caricature of stages now outgrown, reacting to patriarchalist excess by reversion to matriarchalist excess. A new coin comes into sight, different from either side of the old coin we have been tossing about. Really to grasp within ourselves two opposite modes of being, as parts of the whole person we struggle to become, and to accept a similar mixing and meeting in others, means the questions we address one another will increase, in number and intimacy and quality.

Following from this perception of contrasexuality is some awareness of what it means, at bottom, to inquire into one's anima or animus. We know to some degree what happens when we accept the weight of conditioning of our parents and the other early influential figures from whom we gathered our images of our own and the other sex and our ways of acting upon them. We know also with some clarity now the way cultural stereotypes shape our sense of woman and man. What we are only barely coming to know—or perhaps to know again after millennia—is the effect on the ego, both individual and collective, of seeing into the archetypal nature of our own anima or animus. This is extremely difficult to experience and to understand. The language of description for it is almost too subtle. We can miss its revolutionary impact. It is like trying to inquire into the ground upon which we stand, using words like shovels. It is like asking, not about the propositions of our argument, but the premises on which it is based. It is like trying to make explicit the tacit dimensions of our life, like looking directly at the assumptions on which we rest all our cases, which feels in turn like questioning all the bases for our beliefs and actions. It is like seeing the angle of the orienting principle automatically operating in us that positions us in differing degrees of closeness to, and distance from, the center. We see at last the lens through which we focus upon what we are.

Such a vision introduces a gap within us, a useful one, a necessary one. We cannot take for granted any more the certainty of our view. We see our partiality. We cannot depend upon our seeing things right with absolute assurance any more; we see the limitations of our bias. It is to feel the living spirit moving right through us, so radical, so subtle, that everything is taken away at once and just as quickly returned, but no longer the same as it was. What moves us across the threshold into the center, in this viewing and unviewing, in this gap, is our maleness and femaleness. Or to put it more accurately, through our femaleness and maleness we hear the summons, so intimate and so forceful, to respond, to answer that antecedent Being in whose image we are created.

LIMITED ENGAGEMENTS

Philip Turner

I

Not long ago *Newsweek* reported that the 1982 studies of John Kantner and Melvin Zelnick of Johns Hopkins University showed that one out of five girls who had reached the age of fifteen admitted to having had sexual intercourse. By the time these young women had reached the age of sixteen the figure had risen to one in three, and by seventeen, nearly one out of every two.

I note these figures only to make concrete something everyone knows, namely, that sexual activity between unmarried men and women has risen steadily over the past twenty-five years and that it tends to begin at an increasingly early age. These figures were made even more vivid for me during a recent trip to Florida when I stood in line in a convenience store behind a group of two boys and three girls between the ages of thirteen and fifteen and watched as they made a purchase of soda, bubble gum and condoms.

Most parents now simply assume that their children will have sexual relations before they are married. Many believe, at least in respect to older teenagers, that this change in custom represents a social advance that serves to provide a healthy sexual apprenticeship and a means of preventing precipitous marriage.[1] There are many others who do not favor the change, but nonetheless believe that the only thing they can do about it is to caution their children to be careful and responsible in respect to their choice of partner(s) and in the use of effective birth control.

Sexual relations between young men and women in their teens are increasingly common, but, on the whole, they still arouse in us discomfort and sometimes even disapproval. These early sexual relations, however, are but one part of our changing social practice. Indeed, they simply reflect a profound change in the thought and behavior of adults. In all age groups, unmarried men and women, with increasing frequency, enter some form of sexual relation, and American society on the whole now either encourages these relations or accepts them. There may be some residual awkwardness when a couple who live together introduce one another as "my friend," but the awkwardness is often more an expression of social uncertainty than it is one of moral concern.

What Americans do about sex has changed dramatically, but so also has the way we think about it. If no harm is done to either of the individuals or to those close to them, we tend to think that what they do is their own affair. Sex is not a matter of public business. It is rather a matter of private choice, and in this respect we tend to think of sexual relations in the same way we now do most others—as private agreements, the terms of which are to be set only by the parties involved. Thus sex can be for love, or for fun, or for personal growth, or for comfort, or for having a child, or for any other purpose to which the parties involved may agree.

These changes in the ways in which Americans both behave and think have progressed with remarkable speed and they have in the process set up what William Werpehowski has nicely termed "the pathos of Christian ethics today."[2] The pathos is simply that the interests and desires of autonomous individuals now play such an important part in our ethical vision and deliberation that there tends to be little general understanding of the traditional Christian view that people "flourish in and through patterns of relationship that are themselves taken to be normative."[3]

Because the very basis of its traditional teaching has been undermined by these changes in thought and behavior, they have proven enormously painful especially for what are often called the "mainline churches." These churches have until recently thought of themselves as the moral arbiters of the nation, yet the sexual revolution has served as well as anything to demonstrate that the basic moral assumptions which once guided the mainline churches are not widely shared. As a result, they are no longer able to fulfill their traditional role in American society. Their new social circumstances have placed them on the horns of a dilemma. On the one hand, their membership still expects the "denominations" to teach good morals, set a good example, and form character. On the other, the members of the mainline churches themselves have become so fragmented in their social life and so individualistic in their thinking that they tend either to ignore what is often called "the traditional teaching of the church" or to be outraged if a minister or pastor insists that this teaching ought to be binding on their conscience and determinative of their behavior.

Ministers find themselves, as a result of these countervailing forces, in an impossible position. In certain contexts they are expected to defend "traditional teaching" and in all circumstances they are expected to set a good example themselves. Nevertheless they are not to be old-fashioned and "judgmental" when dealing with the people of their congregation who do not live by this teaching or who do not believe it to be a very enlightened opinion. Furthermore, though still expected by some to defend and strengthen the moral fiber of the country, they are not to try to impose their religious and moral beliefs within the general life of society as a whole.

No wonder so many clergy seem to stagger between conflicting opinions and speak out of both sides of their mouths. This same double-mindedness can be found in the deliberations of the governing bodies of their churches. On the one hand, these official bodies feel compelled to speak and teach about sexual morality; on the other, they fear to say anything very clearly because if they do they will be attacked by one group or another from within the church they are meant to teach, lead and govern. They will also be attacked from without by irate critics who will complain about their meddling in what ought rightly to be private business.

Pastors and the members of the governing bodies of their churches are not the only people who have been confused by the sexual revolution. It is fair to say that somewhere most church members, no matter what their stated opinions may be, share the confusion of their pastors and the muddle found within the pronouncements of their churches. A history of 2,000 years during which the church has consistently taught that sexual relations ought to take place only between a man and a woman who are married one to another has left its mark upon the conscience of all, and the voice of that conscience cannot be stilled by a simple act of will, a change of public opinion, a new pattern of social behavior, or a new study by the governing body of a church. The voice of traditional conscience still speaks even if only in the midst of change, revolt or uncertainty.

These observations about the state of our churches and the condition of our souls are intended to make clear that the ethics of sex is in fact a subject which allows us to see into the state of both our corporate and individual lives. It is a mirror in which we can behold ourselves. In order to provide such a looking glass I propose to ask and try to answer one strategic question. Given the fact that the church can no longer serve as the moral arbiter for American society, what ought it to say and do about the fact that not only do most church members not understand the reasons for "traditional teaching," but increasing numbers neither live by this teaching nor hold it to be binding?

I have argued elsewhere that it is unsatisfactory to respond by saying that the church, in order to exert greater social influence and to have a more effective pastoral ministry, ought to change its teaching so as to make it conform more closely with general social practice and common social opinion.[4] Such a strategy is tempting indeed to churches which are steadily losing not only their social position, but also their membership. Nevertheless, such a policy of accommodation will issue not in social and pastoral effectiveness, but in the takeover of the church by a culture that is no longer Christian in its most basic moral assumptions and forms of life.

I have also argued that the dilemma cannot adequately be addressed simply by making room for all sorts of belief and practice.[5] "Inclusivity," the code word now used for such a policy, seeks to make room for difference and escape making punitive judgments, but in its present form speaks for a church that has no center and nothing to recommend save a tolerance that has become, in fact, indifference. If the churches seek to deal with the dilemmas that confront them by saying simply that, as long as differing beliefs are held sincerely and no one is injured by one's actions, sexual ethics are to be considered a purely personal matter, then the churches will cease being churches and become voluntary societies which can be joined for private reasons alone. They will become what Robert Bellah has called "life style enclaves," which make no attempt to shape the beliefs and ways of life of their members but instead seek to be effective vehicles for the satisfaction of personal tastes and private wants.[6]

If it is unsatisfactory either to change for the sake of social and pastoral effectiveness or to say that sexual ethics are now simply a matter for private conscience to decide upon, what is the way ahead? A serious moral question has been raised about the "traditional teaching of the church." Given the prolonged period that now generally precedes marriage and the fact that many people cannot or ought not to marry—including teenagers and young adults, the middle-aged divorced, older widows and widowers—and given that a healthy sex life is such an important aspect of human flourishing, ought not the church to change its teaching? Should it not allow for wholesome and committed sexual relations between people who are not married? This question is a serious one, and I will return to it frequently during the course of the argument that follows.

First, however, let me make clear my belief that the first question to be addressed by Christians in the present debate over sexual ethics is not what will be socially convincing and pastorally effective, nor what will seem "non-judgmental" and tolerant, nor whether sexual abstinence runs contrary to human flourishing, but another question entirely. What ought the church to teach and expect of people who profess to be disciples of Christ? Ought the church to hold up the traditional teaching as marking the way of discipleship, or ought it to say instead that now we have different expectations for the sexual behavior of disciples?

I think that the traditional view is in fact far more adequate an account of the demands of discipleship, marking out a better way toward human flourishing than any of the current proposals for revision. In this chapter I shall attempt to defend this view, arguing that the traditional teaching of the church ought not to be changed. At the same time, however, I will argue that defense of the traditional teaching implies a fundamental reassessment of the nature of the church and its relation to the larger society, along with a thoroughgoing reformation of its common life. Apart from such reassessment and reform, recommendation of the traditional teaching will be unconvincing, ineffective and "moralistic."

II

Can the traditional teaching become more than a ghost from Christmas past come to haunt the conscience and divide the church? Can it in fact become a guide to freedom and a treasure to be shared with all who will listen? These are the questions, but an answer requires first a statement of exactly what the "traditional teaching" is.[7] This teaching is far more complex than most realize and far less understood than most assume, and it is clear that if the church is to up hold the traditional teaching, it will have to take steps to see that it is passed on, understood and adequately recommended to conscience.

The "traditional teaching" as now most commonly understood has its roots in a single biblical metaphor, "one flesh," and this metaphor is intended to concentrate in one image the "ends" or "goods" God is believed to have in mind for both sexual relations and for marriage (Gen. 2:24; Mt. 19:6; Mk. 10:8; Eph. 5:31). In both sexual relations and marriage, the tradition holds that a man and a woman are intended by God to become "one flesh." That is, they are to be joined physically, they are to share a particularly extensive and intensive form of social life, and they are to undertake the procreation, care and nurture of the next generation.[8]

The meaning of "one flesh" as used in its original source, Genesis 2, is extraordinarily complex. It refers to the creation of a complete society in which a man and a woman become related one to another across the full spectrum of possibilities for human relationships. In becoming one flesh a man and a woman form a basic social unit, a family, in which all forms of human exchange may and ought to be practiced. Accordingly, in becoming one flesh, the man and the woman come together in and through sexual relations. They also share a common life and in so doing provide for one another the many and various forms of help which are possible for human beings. Finally, they are one flesh in the sense that they communicate one with another in a particularly close way. It is out of this complex union that children are born and nurtured and the life of society continually formed and renewed.[9]

In all these ways, the man and the woman who become one flesh are neither alone nor helpless. All these meanings are contained within a single image; it is from these meanings that the goods of sex and marriage are derived. Accordingly, the Christian tradition, as it has evolved over the centuries, has held that the goods of sex are pleasure, unity or mutual society, and the procreation of children. Further, the tradition has insisted that the goods of sex are rightly sought only within marriage.

Marriage thus has its own set of goods and, not unexpectedly, they are similar to those of sexual relations themselves. The goods of marriage, the tradition holds, are based in the human need to find help and companionship during the course of life, in the responsibility people have for begetting and caring for the next generation, and in the duty all people share to direct sexual desire to morally acceptable purposes. Given these needs and responsibilities, the tradition holds that the goods of marriage are "unity," "procreation," "a remedy for sin," and "a school of charity."

A fully adequate defense of the traditional teaching must be rooted in each of the goods of marriage. This chapter will tackle only a portion of that task and in so doing focus on the unitive goods of sex and marriage and what they suggest about sexual ethics. A brief word must be said first, however, about the two other goods of marriage. From the beginning, the tradition has insisted that procreation is a divinely intended end or good of sex and that the procreation of children ought not to take place apart from the bond of marriage. Although those who make this claim take full cognizance of the fact that both the procreation and nurture of children may *in fact* take place apart from the marriage bond, they still insist that neither ought to be separated *in principle* from this bond.

The distinction between a separation *in principle* and a separation *in fact* may at first seem both obscure and fussy, but a simple example will show that it is neither. Let us take the case of adoption. In such cases, one or more people stand in for the parents of a child because, for one reason or another, the parents cannot or will not assume their responsibilties. In this case, the nurture of a child is separated in fact from the bond of marriage, but is not so separated in principle. In like manner, an elderly couple who marries may be past the age of child-bearing. In this case, sex and marriage are separated in fact from procreation but not in principle since, if they could have children, the procreation of those children would take place within their marriage bond.

This particular aspect of the traditional teaching deserves more attention. Indeed, one of the strongest arguments for the traditional teaching and against a revision that allows for ecclesial blessings of "committed relationships" is that such a move warrants in principle the separation of love-making and baby-making. As has been pointed out many times, a justification of love-making that has no relation in principle to baby-making suggests the moral probity of baby-making that has no relation to love-making.[10] Once such a separation is allowed in principle, the moral possibilities for the making of children become almost limitless, possibilities traced with gruesome humor by Aldous Huxley in his futurist novel *Brave New World*. It takes only a quick perusal of the headlines with their accounts of surrogacy and *in vitro* fertilization for one to realize that Huxley's future world is a possibility that lies far closer than we might think.

A brief look at the third good of marriage also bears upon our question. By saying that marriage serves as a remedy for sin, the tradition of the church at its worst holds that the "sin" *necessarily* involved in sexual relations is in some way compen-

sated for by the faithfulness involved in the marital relationship. At its best, however, the tradition of the church seeks to
point out that the relation between a man and woman in
marriage directs sexual desire to its proper end and in so doing
serves to remedy the temptation men and women share to
"use" each other for the achievement of selfish ends.

By saying that marriage serves as a school for charity, the
tradition of the church addresses the same problem in a more
positive light, and across a broader spectrum of human experience. It has sought to indicate that the relation between a
man and a woman in marriage can serve to teach them, in all
areas of life, to love as God intends. For those called to it,
marriage can serve as a school wherein we learn, by grace, to
overcome a form of self-love that is both ungodly and humanly
destructive; in so doing we learn greater compliance with the
law of life, namely that we are made to love God with all our
heart, soul, mind and strength and our neighbor as ourselves.
We shall return to the significance of the third good of marriage when we speak later of the virtues or powers of soul
necessary for the realization of love's promise. It is enough to
say at the moment that proposals to revise the churches'
teaching about sexual morality must also cut the moral tie once
thought to exist between sexual relations and the belief that
marriage, precisely in relation to sexual relationships, is intended by God as a remedy for sin or as a school of charity.

Enough has been said to make clear the basic point from
which this and any additional investigations must begin. The
traditional teaching of the church about sexual relations and
marriage is an extended interpretation of the metaphor "one
flesh," and its central tenets are that the goods of sex are not
in principle to be separated one from another, nor are they to

be sought apart from the wider covenant of marriage. According to the traditional teaching, a sexual relation ought not to be entered merely for pleasure or merely for companionship or merely for children. In no way are any of these goods to be *in principle* cut off from the others or sought apart from the abiding relation enjoined by the marriage covenant.

It has been necessary to provide some sketch of the traditional teaching not only because many do not understand its complexity, but also because, apart from it, the various proposals for the revision of Christian sexual ethics will not be adequately grasped. The revisionist proposals now in the field suggest either that one or another of the goods of sex can rightly be sought apart from the others or that the goods of sex, even if kept together, can be sought apart from the goods of marriage. So defense of the traditional teaching amounts to providing reasons which accord not only with Scripture and with the tradition of the Bible's interpretation, but also with the knowledge we have as human beings of the nature of these relationships. When a form of what is sometimes called "reflective equilibrium" between these elements has been reached, we may safely say that an adequate justification has been provided.

Now I want to focus attention on whether or not the knowledge we now have of the nature of sexual relations can provide support for the traditional teaching. I begin at this point and ask this particular question because it is often said that it is precisely our present knowledge and experience of sexual relations that throws the traditional teaching into question. Looked at in this way, the crucial question is not whether the traditional teaching enjoys the support of Scripture and tradition, since I believe it does, but whether or not the view suggested by the Bible receives support from what we know about sexual relations. Can we continue to hold to it without sacrificing both intelligence and personal integrity?

The philosopher Roger Scruton, though not a Christian, has presented, in an extraordinary work entitled *Sexual Desire: A Moral Philosophy of the Erotic*, an account of sexual relations which lends far more credibility to the traditional teaching than it does to the proposals being made for its revision.[11] I want to begin by noting some things he points out about the nature of sexual desire, erotic love and marriage, and by making some comments of my own.

If we ask first of all what it is to desire another person in a sexual way, we quickly become aware that more is involved in sexual desire than animal appetite. If desire were nothing but appetite, we would be able to satisfy it easily and, once satisfied, we would not find ourselves still filled with yearnings we cannot account for.

Though we have been conditioned to think of desire as an expression of animal nature alone, it is easy to show that we are mistaken in this view. Imagine two people who are filled with desire for one another. One of them suddenly finds out that the other has consistently lied to them. What happens to desire? The chances are it will disappear quickly and be replaced by very different feelings indeed. If desire is simply an urge like hunger, would these reactions be common to our experience? I think not.

Sexual desire, to be sure, has roots in the urges of the body, but it is in fact a far more complex response than appetite. Sexual desire is a complex psychological, moral and social phenomenon that shows us to be a good bit more complicated than animal nature alone allows. Sexual desire is a passion that has roots in animality but is nonetheless peculiar to people. Desire represents what Roger Scruton calls "an immense moral labor that might not have occurred."[12] In contrast to simple appetite, sexual desire is an achievement of civilization "which it would be folly to discard and yet which can, like morality, be discarded at almost any time."[13] Animals, he argues, have sexual urges, but only people have sexual desires.

Is what Scruton says in fact true? Think for a moment about the aim of sexual desire. If we desire someone, what is it that we want? Are we simply after a body to relieve the tension we feel in our own? Are we the tools of simple instinct? Do we not rather want to call another person, a particular person, with a name and a face and a distinct personality, into immediate presence in the flesh? Is not our hope that the body we long to have will prove in the end more than a body? Is it not our hope that the one whom we desire will become in a sexual act directly present to us?

What we hope for in our sexual relations is an "incarnation" of the other so that in them flesh and spirit are one. Do we not long for an eclipse of the distance between the heart and the flesh of the one whom we desire so that their heart and flesh become one? And do we not yearn for the two of us, in and through a sexual relation, to be united in a similar way in both heart and flesh?

If the answer to these questions is yes, as I believe it is, then the metaphor of one flesh seems not only to indicate what our sexual relations ought to be like, but also to describe what we *hope* they will be like. It is a metaphor which, if you will, joins what we know to be our duty with what we know to be our desire and in so doing resolves the most profound problem of ethics, namely, how that which is mandatory also becomes desirable.

I do not wish to appear naive. We are not always pure in heart. Our inner state, when possessed by desire, is never simple. Obscenity, lust, perversion and fantasy constantly make us settle for less than the presence of another. These sirens, however, do not always silence the voice of our deepest longing and the fact that anything less than the presence of the other in the flesh leaves us unsatisfied (even when our urges are quiet) indicates what we believe the promise of sexual relations to be. That promise, according to the traditional teaching of the church, is a cure for our loneliness.

At this point, I must note in passing something that will become increasingly important as this argument progresses. The fact that what we long for in sexual relations and what actually occurs are not the same suggests that the fulfillment of sexual desire is not something of which we are equally capable. The ability to be present to another in the flesh and to receive a similar gift from them is not a natural capacity. It is rather a "virtue," a power of soul, which we must somehow come by in the course of living.

I shall say something later about what this power of soul entails and how we come by it, but I must now make clear how this discussion of the nature of desire bears upon a defense of the traditional teaching. Sexual desire leads in many directions, one of which is intimacy. Otherwise we are made extremely uncomfortable, for sexual activity without intimacy seems doubtful to us both in respect to taste and morals. Then, because sexual desire tends to produce and express intimacy, sexual desire also tends to move beyond itself toward something we call love. erotic love shares with sexual desire an interest in the embodiment of another, but it incorporates sexual desire, with its longing for union, into a larger and more difficult project. Erotic love aims not only at union but also at a community that transcends the moment of mutual presence and intimacy which is the end of desire.

The community at which love aims is one in which the particular interests of the two individuals are incorporated into a common set of aims, interests, benefits and burdens. This community of love does not require a merger in which the distinction between the interests of the two parties is erased,[14] but individual interests must be incorporated in a way that gives them new meaning and new importance. In receiving a new meaning, individual interests may either assume a greater or lesser importance. Whichever may be the case, however, they are now determined in relation to a common good.

So it is not only the nature of desire but also of erotic love that is best captured by the image of "one flesh." In respect to erotic love, the unity of one flesh sought by lovers includes, but is more encompassing, than their physical union. Their union takes place in and through a common good and this fact carries with it an implication of enormous moral significance.

Because true lovers seek a common good, it is terribly important that, in entering a love relation, neither is set at war with their deepest convictions, aims and interests. If the joint project love calls forth runs contrary to personal integrity, a possibly unbearable war is set up between what is deepest in the heart and the good sought in the relation. Such a clash is likely to end in either the destruction of love or the destruction of personal integrity or both. In all likelihood it was for a similar reason that Paul urged the Christians at Corinth not to marry unbelievers(I Cor. 6:14; 7:39). Such a union might well set up a conflict between the good of faith on the one hand and the good common to the marriage on the other.

Having made these observations about erotic love, there are two things we must note if we are to grasp adequately their significance. The first is that achievement of the aims of love requires that one be capable both of realizing these aims and of judging the worth of the person one loves, the goals the other has for the relationship, and their own capacity to reach them. Just as the fulfillment of desire requires a certain power of soul, so does fulfillment of the aim of love. If "virtue" is indeed necessary for the fulfillment of the aims of desire and the promise of love, then one must ask how the necessary power of soul to be a successful lover is to be acquired and recognized.

The second point is that achievement of the aim of love requires that lovers be in a relationship that is ongoing. The unity of purpose to which lovers aspire demands frequent exchanges of many sorts. It requires also a degree of understanding and sympathy that can come only from the closest association. Finally these exchanges cannot be skewed in their unitive purpose by the diverting and dividing presence of other parties.

What then do these observations about sexual desire and erotic love suggest in respect to the traditional teaching of the church? Their significance will become obvious if we make one more observation. We have seen that love is more than desire though desire may be included in love. Indeed, when love takes desire into itself, it gives desire the constancy it lacks and saves it from the dangers which most threaten it, namely, a descent into obsession, lust or obscenity. Love makes the moral limitations of desire clearly visible. At the same time, however, even as love serves to promote desire's fulfillment, more than love is needed if it is to succeed in its aims.

Think for a moment of what anyone who is in love knows. Love, in so far as it is love rather than infatuation or a love for love, cannot plan for its own demise. Love has about it what Roger Scruton calls a "nuptial quality"; it cannot be fulfilled and then discarded.[15] Because it is a passion that does not wish or plan for its own death, and requires time and space as well as certain powers of soul for its realization, love, unlike simple desire, looks for a good deal more than emotional sincerity or honesty of intention in its recipient. It hopes for and requires a stronger guarantee of fidelity and permanence than the purity of our feelings or the resolution of our inconstant wills.

Love by nature seeks constancy more than signs of affection or declarations of good intention. For this reason, only something like a vow can give love the surety it seeks. That surety is a place of safety where lovers can rest, knowing that the desire which expresses, feeds and sustains their love will not be allowed to focus its glance elsewhere. In this respect vows do two things. They assure us of constancy and they carry with them the implied pledge that the people who make them will seek those powers of soul necessary for the fulfillment of desire's aim and love's promise.

Vows do still another thing. They locate us within a world of public expectation that is more powerful than our private intentions. Vows place our intentions within the constraining wall of social institutions and by these we are held accountable for what we make of our emotions and our intentions. Our romantic illusions too often blind us to this fundamental truth about ourselves. If our intimacies are to survive, they must receive public recognition and support.

It is not unreasonable, therefore, to conclude that it is within the institution of marriage that erotic love finds its most adequate base for a full flowering. It is the institution of marriage which provides public support for the private space lovers need to go about their business. Secret loves are not noted either for their length or their health, and even when they endure, as they sometimes have, they nonetheless crave a public place in which to sun themselves and breathe healthy air. It is marriage that gives this place.

In marriage, lovers enter a social institution that places them within boundaries larger than those inscribed by their private aims, desires and intentions. What is the nature of the boundaries within which the vows of marriage place us? In entering the "order" or "estate" of marriage, lovers do not, by their vows, make a contract with one another for this or that service. Rather, they enter a relation whose precise duties and responsibilities cannot be either foreseen or predetermined by nuptial contract. The specific demands of marriage derive from what is demanded by a common good, one that exceeds the particular interests of the lovers and whose means of procurement cannot be predetermined or foreseen. Marriage is, therefore, the institution that best provides the public blessing and support required for the success of our most intimate and private undertaking—a community based upon love. Further, if we look for an image that captures the nature of the bond marriage effects and enjoins, "oneflesh" once more serves far better than any other available.

If we look at marriage as we have at desire and love, we find again two strikingly similar things. Marriage, desire and love, each in their own way, can most adequately be described as a relation of one flesh. Further, marriage, like desire and love, is a relationship that demands certain powers of soul for its realization. Not everyone is able to pursue with another a common good and not everyone is able to accept the changes in meaning and importance that consequently occur in respect to their personal aims and private interests. Marriage, like sexual desire and erotic love, requires certain "virtues" and not everyone possesses these necessary powers to an equal degree.

The traditional teaching of the church holds that the chief of these virtues is "chastity." Chastity is a much-abused and now little-used word, but we haven't a better one and it is of crucial importance to grasp the meaning of this word once more if the promises of desire, love and marriage are to be fulfilled. To be sure, according to traditional teaching both married and single people are to be "chaste." What chastity implies for a single person is an important and terribly neglected subject. For married people, chastity requires, at a minimum, the ability to contain desire within the bonds of love and direct it toward the fulfillment of love's purpose. Further, the chaste lover is able to direct love itself in a way that honors the one upon whom it is bestowed. This ability includes the power of soul necessary to be faithful until death to another in both heart and action. Finally, a chaste man or woman has the power of soul necessary to subsume the erotic love that moves them within a greater love, namely a love for God and love for the common good to which God calls them. According to the traditional teaching, unless husband and wife love God above all else, their own union, which lasts only until they are parted by death, will fail to yield its promise and may well turn destructive.

It is now time to see what can be made of this tracing of the links between sexual desire, erotic love and marriage. We have seen that though there is no necessary relation between them, they are nonetheless open one to another. There seems to be in their relation not a necessary connection, but what Scruton has called a "vector" or direction of movement. Each points to the other. Desire, love and marriage remain discrete: neither turns into the other, yet each needs something beyond itself in order to be fulfilled. As one moves from sexual desire to love and then to marriage, the meaning of "one flesh" becomes more and more complex, while the increasing complexity of the relationships signified by this metaphor calls for increasingly complex powers of soul for their realization.

For Christians, the metaphor of one flesh gains additional force when we take note of another relationship in which we speak of two being united in "one flesh." This "union" of two in one has been taken over the ages to provide a moral and religious paradigm for the relation Christians ought to have with self, others and God. It is particularly illuminating in the case of sexual relations.

I speak of the relation between God and the man Jesus. The unity of God with the life of a human being in Christ is of a sort that our sexual unions ought to image. Christ is the Word made flesh. In Christ we see the image of God, and we do so because the distance between the heart and flesh of the man Jesus is vacated, as is the distance between his heart and flesh and the heart of God. Furthermore it is God in Christ who makes us part of the body inhabited upon earth by his Spirit. God's intention for our body and for the life of that body we call the church is that, in both, the distance between heart and flesh be vacated so that the glory of God can be seen in the life, which is to say the body, which is ours and which is that of the church.

It is the analogy that exists between the unity possible for a man and a woman in marriage and the unity between God and Christ and between Christ and the church that allows the author of the Epistle to the Ephesians to call marriage a great "mystery," a manifestation of God's plan for all people. That plan is not for everyone to marry but it is for God to become one flesh with each man and woman as he does in the life of the man Jesus.

What moral imperative is suggested by this analogy? What is suggested by these tracings of a vector between sexual desire, erotic love and marriage, as well as the interpretation of this vector by the image of two becoming "one flesh"? It suggests that there is good reason to hold that the traditional teaching both enunciates the sexual good of all people and marks out the way of discipleship for those called into a sexual relation. Such a conclusion accords not only with Scripture, but also with what we know about sexual desire, erotic love and marriage. Thus, what is commanded by God coheres with what we know to be our good. God's call to discipleship does not call us away from ourselves but more fully into the depths of our nature. As in all adequate schemes of Christian believing, grace does not destroy nature but restores and perfects it.

The tracing we have made of the connection between desire, love and marriage and the investigation we have carried out concerning the meaning of "one flesh" suggests another thing as well. The best way to cultivate the powers of soul necessary if sexual desire, erotic love and marriage are to have their promise fulfilled is to maintain the moral connections between them and to refuse, as revisionists propose, to allow one or another of them to be pursued independently. To the extent that we pursue these goods independently of one another, the powers of our souls are trimmed back, abridged, diminished or simply left undeveloped.

III

Even if the argument to this point is plausible, there are still good reasons to press the question further. Why, even if there is a directional flow between sexual desire and erotic love and marriage, is there a moral requirement to keep these states (and the activities they engender) together? The transformation of appetite into desire and the linkage of desire, love and marriage are, after all, events that have occurred in the course of history. They are the products of both nature and culture, not of nature alone. They have not always been linked as they are in our mind and experience and perhaps they ought not to remain so.

This observation exposes the heart of all revisionist positions. The basic argument for revision of the traditional teaching, though it may take many forms, is this. There is a distinct good in sexual desire and its fruition in freely entered and non-injurious sexual acts, just as there are distinct goods in the more wide-ranging relations of erotic love and/or marriage. Why not treat these goods as discrete, even if related, and allow their pursuit in isolation one from another? What harm is done? Is not real good prevented and real harm done by such a morally ambitious linkage? Is the traditional teaching not an ethic for "over-achievers"? Why foist such scrupulosity on others?

The answer in each case is that to make, *in principle*, a moral separation between sexual desire, erotic love and marriage places in jeopardy the full promise of each at the same time that it exposes each to distortion and moral abuse. Suppose, for example, we were once again to say that marriage ought to be separated in principle from sexual desire and erotic love? Such a moral state is certainly the most common we have known through the course of history and we ought not to forget that it took a long time, even within the Christian tradition, to get desire, love and marriage linked in a moral way. What would it be like to return to those "exciting days of yesteryear" when marriage did not have a necessary moral relation to desire and love?

Would we think of such a return as a moral advance? We would, I think, on the contrary, hold it to be a moral retrogression. In the first place, marriage would be stripped of two of its most attractive goods; in the second, the man and the woman would become increasingly useful to one another for social purposes (like wealth, prestige offspring or security) that lie beyond their common good.

It is not, however, the proposal to separate marriage from desire and love that has the greatest attraction within our society, but the separation of desire from love and desire and love from marriage. Both these proposals illustrate the same point I have just made: both place in jeopardy the promise of the relations in question and make it more than likely that either the man or the woman will be abused in some way.

What is going on when, in a state of desire, we seek to call another person to an immediate presence in the flesh? What does it mean if we claim that the call we issue need not be motivated by love nor have love in any way in view? Does not such a moral stance skew the very direction in which desire leads? And what can be the motive for issuing such a call once its moral connection with love has been severed? Is not the motive likely to be either a vain curiosity on the one hand or a very personal and highly self-referential need on the other?

The ethic that is enjoying increasing popularity in church circles is one which makes a moral separation between sexual desire and erotic love on the one hand, and marriage on the other. The most common version of this proposal holds that if people truly desire each other and are "in love" and if there is "commitment" in their relationship, then sexual relations are morally permissible apart from the vows that convert erotic love into a permanent and exclusive union. The essence of this proposal, which is the strongest of the revisionist arguments now current, is that sexual relations ought to be loving and faithful but they need not be permanent.

There are two points at which this view requires careful assessment, and the first concerns the nature of the relation that is supposed to link the lovers involved. Looked at from one angle, it appears to rest upon the premise that the relation in question is a test and only a test. No matter how passionate, the relation is an uncertain one; within it, sex becomes a part of the way in which both love and the loved one are examined. In either case, sexual relations are part of an experiment.

Looked at from another point of view, the relation may appear as part of an exchange where each person is after something, but is unwilling to make a permanent or exclusive commitment to get it. The agreement is "for the time being" and for limited purposes—for pleasure and sexual release, or for warmth and emotional satisfaction, or simply the company of a helpful companion. From each point of vantage a different set of meanings may appear, but from all points of view the lovers in question are involved in a limited engagement: a calculation of benefits and burdens, a test of feelings, and, most of all, a deliberate assessment of the possibility or advisability of love's demise.

So not only must we assess the nature of the relationship, but also the character of the lovers. They are to be "committed," but what is the meaning of this description of their intentions and motives? Commitment is at root a power of soul—I take this virtue to be a modern substitute for chastity. A revision of this magnitude of the traditional account of sexual virtue deserves careful scrutiny. Careful scrutiny, however, is just what the word "commitment" has not received from its advocates. If one reads the literature carefully and asks exactly what the moral requirements of "commitment" are, it is in the end very difficult to say.

A recent article in a denominational newspaper spoke of "committed sexual relationships" as ones in which two people undertake for periods of "varying duration" to share their lives in "a mutually responsive, loving way."[16] James Nelson in his widely read book *Embodiment* says that the church ought to provide "guidelines" for people "who do not see marriage or remarriage as an expression of their vocation, and yet do not intend a life of complete celibacy."[17] The first of the guidelines he provides is "commitment." Nelson goes on to say that a committed relationship that it should manifest "a profound respect for the other as a person, a deep caring for the partner's well-being . . . . marked by honesty and the concern for social responsibility. In a word, it should embody openness to life."[18] Elsewhere Nelson insists that committed sexual relations embody love, care, trust, openness and fidelity.

These are all recognizable words and they can also be found in association with the word chastity. If we ask more precisely what they involve in their new setting, however, it becomes clear that within "committed relationships" love and care are limited in both extent and duration, and that fidelity, at least in Nelson's account, does not absolutely preclude other sexual partners. Trust and openness are both guarded and subject to frequent reevaluation.

Commitment seems to refer basically to emotional sincerity and to a morally serious dedication to testing the quality of an erotic relationship. It is a virtue, in short, well suited to a limited engagement and as such is a power of soul appropriate for people whom Dante called "trimmers." Commitment, as opposed to chastity, is the expression of a soul that at its deepest level blows neither hot nor cold. It is a virtue for the tentative, one that calls to mind the image of someone testing the water of a bath by sticking their toe in. It is an questionable virtue that makes one wonder if W. H. Auden was not right when he said in his "Christmas Oratorio," "Love's not what she used to be."[19]

Auden's comment appears to be quite accurate. These limited engagements in which desire, love and marriage are separated in principle one from another place in jeopardy the relationship which is the most fully human and the one which we most highly prize, namely, erotic love itself. The danger is twofold. In the first place, love's promise is severely endangered and the sort of relationship love requires is opened to abuse and distortion. In the second place, the power of soul necessary if sexual desire, erotic love and marriage are to yield their promised blessing is "trimmed," or "abridged." The results of this abridgment both of the extensiveness of love's relation and of the power of soul necessary for the support of that relation, indeed mean that "love's not what she used to be."

The subject matter of all human ethics concerns not only the forms of human relationship, but also the powers of soul necessary for successful engagement in those relationships. In both ways, the proposals for revision of the churches' traditional teaching are not only inadequate but on the whole injurious to the very relation they are supposed to further. The subject matter of Christian ethics concerns the way in which God in Christ can be imaged in the various forms of human relationship and in the powers of soul which sustain and generate them. In this respect also the suggestions for revision seem inadequate, presupposing a kind of qualified fidelity and permanence that does not image Christ.

IV

What attitude ought Christians to take toward these increasingly frequent, though limited, sexual engagements? One thing the proponents of revision rightly fear is the sort of judgmental and punitive attitude so characteristic of church life in America and so well depicted in Hawthorne's *The Scarlet Letter*. Descendants of Hester Prynne still fill the land. Critics of the traditional teaching of the church fear not only the self-righteousness that punished her, but also the damage this self-righteousness continues to inflict upon both individuals and the church as a whole.

But need the proponents of the traditional view be self-righteous and punitive? Its defenders can be neither if they understand the teaching rightly; if they do, they will know that before God none of them is chaste. The story of the crowd gathered around the woman taken in adultery is the story of what all Christians are supposed to know about themselves. There is no one who is fully chaste and there is no one who loves as God wills. None can cast the first stone because none is without guilt.

Central to Christian belief is the view that the greatest sin of all is to focus on the faults of others while ignoring one's own. The traditional teaching about sexual relations can be understood properly only within the context of the Christian doctrine of the justification of the sinner by grace through faith. Self-righteousness is thus not a necessary companion of the traditional teaching, but rather a sure sign that it has not been properly understood.

There is another concern revisionists have, however, that is far more serious. They fear that the traditional view does not take into account the very genuine good that is often involved in the "committed relationships" they support. This point recently was made with great force by the mother of a young man, who said to me, "I thank God every day for the woman my son lived with during college. She healed a wound in him." Unspoken was the mother's conviction that the wound lay beyond her own care.

The question is therefore bound to arise: if such good can come, why not give moral license to the relationship that brings it? It is this question that exposes a place at which the traditional teaching requires a more thorough exposition than it has yet received. Can a place be found within it for the obvious good that is part of many of the limited sexual engagements we have been discussing?

Looked at in one way, no place can be found. If we take the traditional teaching *only* as a *command* given by Christ to his disciples, then we must simply say that limited sexual engagements, what we now call "committed relationships," represent a form of disobedience. If the committed relations of which the revisionists speak are viewed *only* in terms of command and obedience, they will inevitably be judged *only* in a negative light.

There is good reason to say that some disobedience is involved in these relationships. Nevertheless, there is another aspect of the traditional teaching that displays these relations in a different and more positive way than the image of command and obedience allows, and it also must be taken into account if a fully adequate moral assessment is to be made. This aspect of the tradition speaks of *good* rather than of command and obedience. It depicts in some detail and with great appreciation the goods of the various aspects of sexual relations, those associated with sexual desire and its fulfillment as well as with the wider and more encompassing relation of erotic love. These goods are, to be sure, abridged and placed in jeopardy when sexual desire, erotic love and marriage are not held morally together. Nevertheless, the goods themselves do not disappear.

It is precisely because the goods of sex and erotic attraction need not be totally eclipsed, even in the most tentative and limited of relationships, that defenders of the churches' traditional teaching demonstrate that they have not understood their own position if they speak only of disobedience. For the traditional teaching, properly understood, implies that we may in fact find some trace of good in the most unlikely of sexual relations. Furthermore, when coupled with an adequate account of Christian believing, the traditional teaching allows us to rejoice whenever and wherever we see good, no matter how minimal or fragile it appears or how tentative and limited the relation in which it is found. Thus one may rejoice in good even when it is seen within a relation that may, for one reason or another, not be right.

To take pleasure in the good another enjoys, however, does not mean that one must close one's eyes to what is deficient, wrong or even evil, or give up the belief that there is a better way. A person with what we may call a "traditional conscience" can, with a good heart, recognize whatever good is to be found in "committed sexual relations" and give thanks for its presence. And yet, they can and indeed ought to insist that the relation in question, no matter what good it may involve, is nonetheless wrong; it is part of the broad rather than the narrow way in which Christ calls his disciples to follow.

Furthermore, they can make these claims even if choosing the narrow path involves refusal of a "committed relation" and, with that refusal, the loss of a much-desired and much-needed good—perhaps even healing or comfort. They can make this wrenching claim because of another belief, one which displays the very foundation upon which traditional conscience rests. It is the belief that God does not call us in a way that does us final harm, nor ask of us more than we are able to bear. The way of the cross is in fact a way of blessing, despite all indications to the contrary. Indeed, Christianity is defined by the belief that in and through the cross of Christ God displays his power to heal and comfort us even in the most extreme of life's circumstances, and even if the cure and comfort he offers involve the infliction of more wounds.

The mother's comment which began this discussion raises in an very immediate way the abiding question of the relation between good, right and happiness. The question is one that cannot be avoided by either theological or philosophical ethics.

Looked at in one way, the history of both may be understood as the history of this debate.

No matter what the conclusions of moral philosophy may be, however, Christian theology cannot remain consistent with itself if ever it claims that the Christian life involves no sacrifice of a deficient good or temporary happiness. Many goods and much happiness must be passed by if the way to the source of all human good and all human happiness is to be followed. What Christian theology must insist upon, however, is that, in following this way, the loss of good does not mean the loss of blessing or fullness of life. Even in the loss that occurs, joys are present which exceed it. This is the meaning of one of the most enigmatic and difficult of Christ's sayings, namely, "All these things will be added unto you."

The mother's comment with which I began this discussion leaves us with another question, however, and the remarks I have made to this point do not address it adequately. Even if the traditional teaching allows us both to recognize the good in "committed sexual relation" and to continue at the same time to recommend the traditional teaching, what are we to say to the young man who may have quite deliberately chosen not to follow it? Despite justifiable fears of appearing overly harsh, it may well be appropriate both to say that the traditional teaching marks a better way and to attempt to convince him that what one says is indeed the case. It may also be appropriate to warn him of the moral and religious dangers involved in such a relationship.

There is, however, one more thing that may also be appropriate. It is to tell him that even in choosing the goods he has, these goods will, in the end, yield their full benefit only if he does not lose sight of the full description of sexual good the traditional teaching traces. In respect to his life as a sexual being, this teaching displays his good, while the fulfillment of his and everyone else's sexual good depends upon it. Thus, if the traditional teaching is kept in mind as the way in which we, as sexual beings, are meant to follow, then the abridged and fragile goods he now enjoys will not later be lost. Rather, they may well take on a fuller meaning and provide the basis for future blessing long after the relation in question is over.

Thus defenders of the traditional teaching need not deny or disparage the genuine goods that come from the various forms of limited sexual engagement our society now allows. In fact they are in a better position than the revisionists to make some lasting sense out of them, since the former are able to show that the goods enjoyed depend upon the traditional teaching for the full extent of their meaning and the full extent of the happiness they can bring. They can also look more realistically at the character of these relations and see both their deficiencies and their dangers.

There are, however, two other ideas that the traditional conscience must grasp more adequately if it is to understand the beliefs that inform it. First, the traditional teaching is intended to shape the life of a community and not that of an individual alone. The traditional teaching presupposes certain things about the nature of the community essential to its power to direct the conscience and its ability to mark the way to good and happiness. The most fundamental of these presuppositions states that "in Christ," within the community of the church, we become members of a "family" or "household" which serves in part as "a cure for loneliness." In Christ, Christians believe that it is no longer necessary to marry in order to escape loneliness. Baptism into Christ provides what once was provided only by marriage, and it is partly for this reason that the early Christians took the unprecedented step of saying that the single state was as honorable as the married one and perhaps even preferable.

Once baptized, each person is given both family and friends in such a way that the terrible problem of human loneliness is, in principle, overcome by incorporation into God's family. Furthermore, because God, in Christ and through the presence of the Holy Spirit, is with us in a particularly close way within this family, the most terrible loneliness of all is, again in principle, overcome. The loneliness in question is the feeling of being alone in the universe.

To the extent that the church recommends its traditional teaching and yet at the same time fails to be a family in which loneliness is remedied, it will fail to recognize the necessary framework for understanding its own teaching. What is more, it will also fail to address the issue which stands behind the fact that so many people now enter sexual relations they know will not last and which they know to contain a very diminished good. The result will be that the traditional teaching will lack power to convince conscience.

Most people are not promiscuous, but they are lonely. Most are not the slaves of uncontrollable urges, but they are desperate for human warmth, comfort and companionship. For many such people, "a committed relationship" is in all likelihood not all they want, but it is perhaps the best they can get. It will almost certainly appear sadistic for someone to say to them, "What you are doing is contrary to the teaching of the church" if at the same time the very church to which they appeal is not a community where family and friends without number may be found. Often it is little more than a collection of lonely individuals no different from the one being given unwelcome moral instruction.

The sexual ethics of Christians ought not to be separated from their understanding of the church, for then the teaching of the church becomes not a way to form a rich and common life, but an abstract principle, or a club with which to beat self and others, or an outrageous limitation upon human freedom, need and desire. Then rejection is an understandable and even fitting response.

It is my belief that the battle over sexual ethics now raging within the churches will not be settled until the question of the nature of the church itself is resolved. Anyone who seeks to defend the traditional teaching is required by the implications of their own position to say that, in this era, an issue far deeper than sexual ethics confronts us. It is the absence of a community of Christians in which no one need be alone. The deep issue is not sex but the constitution of the church and, beyond that, the renewal of society as a whole. The social renewal called for is analogous to that required of the church. What we need to form is a moral and political community which is something more than a lonely crowd in pursuit of private ends. I point to the need for both an ecclesial and social renewal for the simple reason that the current sexual ethics of our society are precisely those of a lonely crowd, and, as far as I can tell, the arguments for revision of the churches' traditional teaching, despite their several differences, are in fact recommendations for the church to adapt itself to the ways of the crowd that surrounds it.[20]

This observation suggests the second point traditional conscience must grasp more adequately than before. The church's teaching about sexual relations can be understood only as part of an entire way of life, one best depicted as a constant process of death and resurrection: death to an idolatrous love of self and resurrection to a new life marked by love of God and love of neighbor. This process of death and resurrection is in fact a process of growth in Christ, a process of moving deeper and deeper into the mystery of God's life and the love that characterizes that life. Anyone who takes this view will be likely to see in the virtue of chastity, and the practice of engaging in sexual intercourse only within the bond of marriage, an indication of divine intent. Accordingly they will hold that there is a divinely intended order for sexual relations that both reflects God's love and serves best to promote human good. The call to follow Christ does not come apart from a call to honor God—both in his person and in his will for human life. Thus the struggle to follow Christ will not take place apart from the struggle to honor what Christians have always believed to be God's intention for the order of human relationships.

If they are to be chaste, both single and married people must learn to love God with all their heart, soul, mind and strength. Marriage is a school of charity, but, before God, so is all of life. The red thread that ties each and every life together is God's relentless struggle to teach us to love rightly, and in this struggle we are required by God to leave certain projects very dear to us behind in order to honor God and follow the way that Providence beckons and the Spirit leads.

Following Christ is what disciples do in order to learn what living "in Christ" is all about. The way in which he leads is characterized by the New Testament as being narrow rather than wide. To follow "the way" requires nothing less than giving over everything to God, and so it is aptly called "the way of the cross." The sacrifice of limited sexual engagements by single people can be understood only as part of God's relentless battle for possession of the human heart, and the expression of a grateful heart of honor and love for God.

If chastity and abstinence are spoken of apart from God's own wooing and our own honoring of God, they appear immediately as priggish, punishing and unwarranted demands made by a code of conscience disconnected from life's deepest longings. Apart from a primary focus upon God's ardent pursuit of each human spirit, our own longing for God and our life together in Christ, the traditional teaching becomes an appalling form of moralism.

Because the traditional teaching has too often been presented apart from an account of God's love for us, and our consequent love for God and each other, too frequently it has become just what its critics claim—namely, a law that restrains our worst impulses at a terrible price. If, however, the traditional teaching is placed within the call of God to return his love with all our heart, soul, mind and strength, the sacrifices required along the narrow way become, by grace, occasions for joy. This is the testimony of the saints through the ages and it is also the testimony of Christ, who prayed just before the sacrifice of his very life that "they may have my joy fulfilled in themselves" (John 17:13b).

TWO SHALL BECOME ONE

Helen Oppenheimer

A remarkably satisfactory definition of marriage is its definition in English law: "The voluntary union for life of one man and one woman to the exclusion of all others."[1] It is almost a paraphrase of the biblical pronouncement that "a man shall leave his father and his mother and be joined to his wife, and the two shall become one" (Gen. 2:4; Mk. 10:7; Eph. 5:31), and, like that pronouncement, so emphasizes the uniting of man and woman that it leaves the question of progeny alone. We are perfectly well aware that the biological function of sexual union is to continue the human race, and that marriage has evolved for the sake of protecting human young in their long infancy. Christians are also well aware that the command to be fruitful and multiply and the blessing of God on human fertility go back to the beginnings of our tradition. But this emphasis has been overworked down the centuries and has contributed to serious distortions of Christian sexual ethics.

Besides adding to the sufferings of childless people, the notion that sex in human beings finds its only purpose and justification in completing the number of God's elect has created enormous amounts of needless guilt about the pleasures of sex. From that has followed, quite naturally, rebellion, and the glorification of the pleasures of sex in their own right. So on both sides the value of sexual relationship as a foundation for personal relationship has gone by default. Within marriage, relationship has been swamped by progeny; without, it has been lost in temporary pleasure. This gloomy picture is not the whole truth, but it has been too large a part of the whole truth. So we may be thankful for definitions of marriage, legal and theological, which redress the balance by putting the emphasis on the union of husband and wife.

We do well to be encouraged by the concept of "one flesh." Without belittling parenthood, we can be allowed to give due importance to the relationship of husband and wife as both physical and personal. Human beings are embodied creatures, animal and spiritual. The institution of marriage is founded upon this double character of human nature. On the one hand, for men and women, their physical union is more than a merely biological activity: we cannot omit the fact that it has something to do with love. Nor on the other hand can we take married love as a purely spiritual affinity of souls, needing no bodily expression.

The Christian faith with its central doctrine that God commended his love towards us by taking human flesh has always, when it would, been well placed to emphasize the wholeness of body and spirit. In our century that emphasis seems particularly congenial and is being reflected in positive accounts of sexual ethics which make the "one flesh" union central and take good heed of its physical basis.[2] To make marriage the paradigm for thinking about the ethics of sex makes chastity positively intelligible as an aspect of fidelity rather than negatively repressive.

It seems ungrateful to go on at once to say that there is a risk here of beginning to prove too much. One's favorite theory occupies the whole of one's vision, so that one comes to forget that there is much more to human life, and much more to Christian theology, than can be seen through this particular window. It is becoming increasingly important to realize this without going back on the ground that has been gained. What we need is a critique which will welcome positive, hopeful developments without making them the be-all and end-all. But first the negative attitudes must be decisively repudiated.

The Christian church has never quite dared to give a wholly adverse account of the marriage union; but it has to be admitted that between fear of our physical natures and admiration for single-hearted celibate love of God, the love of a man and a woman for each other has too often seemed an inadequate or even dangerous second-best. Avoidance of sin has been more in evidence than glorifying God. So, except for the privilege of populating the world, married people have had too little encouragement from the church to rejoice in their blessings. Even the teaching of the Lord has been presented as a law against divorce rather than a charter for faithful pair-bonds.

Yet it is fair to say that a positive understanding of marriage itself, not only for the sake of the procreation of children, has never disappeared, but has remained a thin but strong thread in the tangles of Christian thinking. The great comparison of married love, in the Epistle to the Ephesians, to the love of Christ for the church (Eph. 5:32), has been a notable protection against negatively ascetic presuppositions. Admittedly, rigorists have adopted this theology and elaborated a stern theory of the absolute indissolubility of sacramental wedlock whatever the human circumstances, on the basis of Christ's total faithfulness to the church. Admittedly feminists must read this passage with some suspicion, when what has been picked out of it down the centuries has been the asymmetrical subordination of wife to husband. But underneath all the legalism and authoritarianism the love of husband and wife has never been completely submerged. "There is no relationship between human beings," writes St. John Chrysostom, "so close as that of husband and wife, if they are united as they ought to be." He expatiates warmly on the love of Isaac for Rebecca: "Who would not have loved such a woman, so virtuous, so beautiful, so hospitable, generous and kind, so brave in her soul and vigorous in her body?"[3]

This human love can claim to be theologically grounded as far back as the creation stories. It is not tendentious to affirm that it is this positive tradition, expressed in the concept of the "one flesh" union, which the Lord took up and gave afresh to the church (Mk. 10:6-8), and that the Christian theology of marriage at its best has been based upon this tradition. But there is still plenty of room for controversy about what this "one flesh" union means and about the significance of male and female as made in the image of God.

Recent developments have been happily constructive, and for that very reason need proper scrutiny. We may at least allow ourselves to take hold of the idea that the Genesis stories have really very little to do with Darwin, *anti* or *pro*. The main point about Adam is not the history of the shaping of a full-grown man out of clay and then a woman from one of the man's ribs. The point is that humankind, which is what "Adam" means, takes its origin in God's purpose. Christians have been intrigued by the plural form in the story in Genesis 1: "Let us make in *our* image" (vv. 2-7).[4] Is this an inspired glimpse of the doctrine of the Trinity? It hints anyway that the likeness of humanity, male and female, to the Creator, can be grounded in its capacity for relationship.

Because the theology of creation and the theology of marriage have been found usefully to illuminate each other, enthusiasm can overdo this connection. The result can even be a kind of shrinkage, in which both marriage and creation seem to become something less than they really are. On the one hand, because Christian belief sheds light on the meaning of marriage, it is made to look as if people have to be believers for Christians to recognize them as truly married. On the other hand, even more oddly, because human relationships are able to shed light on the affirmation that humankind is made in the image of God, the doctrine of creation seems sometimes to be reduced to a statement which is all about matrimony. If we are to benefit from these insights we shall need to make some clear distinctions.

Using Words Carefully

We may well say of the theology of marriage what G. F. Woods said of natural law, "All the words which are used are as elusive as goldfish in a bowl. They are most satisfying when no effort is made to handle them."[5] This chapter is an attempt to handle some of the slippery words being used today in discussing what marriage is and should be: partnership, covenant, relationship, union, persons, sacrament.

We can start with a simple example. The concept of *partnership* as a way of characterizing the true nature of marriage is appealing to Christians who are ashamed of the notions of male dominance with which "Christian marriage" has been beset, but who have no wish to jettison or undermine our tradition. "Partner," said Karl Barth encouragingly, "is perhaps the best modern rendering for the term 'helpmeet'."[6] Unfortunately it may be too late to lay claim to "partnership" as what we have always meant by marriage. "Partner" is being widely used as synonym for "bedfellow" in contexts where it is convenient not to indicate whether people are married or not, from advertisements for mattresses to advice on contraception. When "partnership" is brought into discussions of marriage, it may be for the purpose of indicating a secular contrast to religious assumptions.

For instance, "the evolution of marriage as a partnership from its origins as sacramental relationship is now almost complete," say the authors of an interesting and sensitive book about the unhappiness of divorce.[7] They seem to assume that partnership notions and sacramental notions belong to quite different ways of thinking. If Christians want the concept of partnership as part of a theological understanding of marriage they will have to explore its meaning more thoroughly, and at least dissociate it from the kind of business partnership which can be conveniently and painlessly dissolved.

A good corrective to over-businesslike contractual notions of marriage has been found in the profoundly biblical idea of *covenant*. This concept, moreover, can be happily applied to marriage: in a covenant, an *initiative* creates a *relationship* by means of an *oath*, in which two become one and are enabled to keep the *commandment* and receive the *blessing*.[8]

In contrast to "contract," "covenant" sums up a position which is both liberal and thoroughly traditional. Yet, rather surprisingly, the covenant idea can also turn out to face two ways. It can be presented as permissive, not traditional. Ethicist Philip Turner describes the covenantal understanding of marriage as a notion brought in by the Reformers, in contrast to scholastic theories of an indissoluble sacramental bond. "The root metaphor," he says, "of this Protestant view was one of relation rather than substance or being, and this change in metaphors allowed for the view to emerge that divorce was permissible if the covenant was broken or if its end of society proved impossible to achieve."[9] So once again the onus is on Christians who want to use the notion of "covenant" to make it plain which way the emphasis is going.

There is a similar though more complicated story to be told about *relationship*, an even more slippery word which has been at the heart of recent controversies, pressed in to use both for commendation and for disparagement. On the one hand we are recommended to look on marriage as personal relationship rather than as just the way to continue the race or as legalized sex. The notion of "relationship" has been notably put to use lately in repudiation of impersonal legalistic concepts of the meaning of marriage. Against legalism, relational ideas have been notably successful. "The mutual help, society and comfort that the one ought to have of the other" have never been more thoroughly appreciated. But on the other hand "relationship" is far from having things all its own way. One is accused of holding a "merely" relational view instead of believing in a real "ontological" bond. Some disentanglement, both of meaning and of history, is badly needed.

First, "relationship" can signify several overlapping but different ideas. "Personal relationship", especially in education, is used, not very accurately, as a euphemism for "sex and the facts of life." Or, contrariwise, relationships that are personal can be contrasted with sexual encounters that are merely physical and transient. Often "personal relationships" means "warm, human relationships," as opposed to formal official dealings with other people. Or "my personal relationships" can indicate my domestic life as distinct from my career and my duties as a citizen. Women are supposed to deal with personal relationships, men with public affairs. Or "a relational view of marriage" can be held in contrast to an assumption that marriage is simply for the procreation of children. "Marriage as relationship" can mean "marriage as a partnership of equals" rather than a dynastic arrangement or a form of sexual or domestic exploitation. Or "marriage as relationship" can mean "marriage for love," losing its point and maybe becoming voidable if love dies. Or "the relationship of marriage" can be used in quite a neutral way to mean "the upshot of a wedding," the state of life into which the spouses enter, whatever that actually is. There is no need to select just one of these meanings and renounce all the others, so long as they are not allowed simply to mingle. We need to keep asking ourselves what contrast we are drawing.

We could say a good deal about relationship without being committed to any idea that personal relationships are bound to be satisfying. The Church of England's Homily on Holy Matrimony might be said to take a "relational" view of marriage. It starts promisingly with a definition that puts relationship first among the "ends" of marriage. Matrimony is "instituted of God, to the intent that man and woman should live lawfully in perpetual friendship. . . ." But the picture of the marital relationship which the homily goes on to give is of "chidings, brawlings, tauntings, repentings, bitter cursings, and fightings."[10] The main advice it offers, both to husband and wife, is to put up with anything for the sake of peace. One can only be surprised that it took over three centuries more for the escape-route of divorce to become available for such unhappy unions.

So, logically, one can look on marriage as a matter of relationship and yet deny that personal fulfillment has anything essential to do with the meaning of the marriage bond. One could subordinate the interests of the wife entirely to the will of her husband, or the interests of both to the claims of their progeny; and these would be ways of filling in the content of marital relationship though they would hardly be what we usually mean by "relational" or "personalist" views of marriage. But it would be disingenuous to deny that the purpose of this argument is at least to keep open the door to a personalist understanding of the marriage union and an emphasis on "persons in relation." The discussion is not intended eventually to remain neutral, but positively to support a "personalist" view once such a view has been carefully explained.

The story, as so often, is the story of a swinging pendulum. If one looks back to the earlier years of the twentieth century one finds a remarkable rigidity in Christian teaching on marriage, not least in the Church of England. The emphasis was being put upon obedience to the commandments of Christ, understood as law, however harsh the impact might be upon individuals. The voices that were raised on behalf of making people happy seemed simply contrary to what the Bible clearly said.

What began to prevail over this loyal but legalistic certainty was a more flexible emphasis upon relationship and response, grounded not in a few disputable texts but upon the breadth of the New Testament teaching. Surely what the Gospels are really about is personal relationships with God and one another? Here was the key to unlock Christian morality without opening the floodgates to permissiveness. A quarter of a century later it seems worth bearing witness to the sense of discovery, of progress and of fresh insights one had in being seized by these ideas. They were not new to the twentieth century, but certainly seemed to be characteristic of it. A personalism which laid stress on persons *in relation* seemed in tune with Christian teaching about love and with humanist concern for people. For Christians the significance of human relationships depends upon our fundamental relationship with God, the ultimate Person. But personalist Christians can happily find that up to a point their contemporaries who do not believe in God are talking the same language. There is quite a lot of "personalism" left even when it is not completed by belief in a personal God. The application to marriage is particularly promising. If relationships matter at all, they certainly matter in marriage.

What many of us have hoped is that Christians and unbelievers could wage war on legalism together, in search of a morality of response, rather than of impersonal law which does not touch people's hearts. The point that legalism misses and the emphasis on relationship promises to correct is that law as such is external. Faithfulness that is commanded as a matter of obedience is a mechanical kind of faithfulness. If people are to put their hearts into doing what they ought they need more than telling, they need enabling. Real faithfulness is a response to something given. Love, whether divine or human, draws out love better than the authority of duty.

Christians who believe in "justification by faith" understand the religious meaning of this emphasis on response. We love because God first loved us. Moralists who make "relationship" the key to what makes human life worthwhile are feeling after a kind of secular application of "justification by faith." We love because other people first loved us. Love draws out reciprocal love, at all levels.

So Christians have sought to illuminate their doctrine of marriage by drawing upon contemporary psychological understanding of how people interact with one another. Much of the current discussion in the Church of England goes back to a series of church reports which addressed the problems of marriage and divorce, such as the Root Report of 1971, followed by the more substantial—though not unanimous—Lichfield Report in 1978. The authors of these reports were far from being trendy radicals. Their loyalty was to traditional teaching, but they did not suppose that the tradition could be simply upheld by legislation. They gave prominence to relational ideas which complicate the straightforward "thou shalt not" of legalism, pointing that the limited concept of contract does little justice to Christian marriage, a state which the Second Vatican Council calls a community of love. One writer argued for the scriptural roots of the notion that marriage is above all a relationship, an idea upheld "in the notion of the covenant and St. Paul's analogy of Christ and the Church. It is in this sense of relationship and community that Christian marriage can be understood more fully in all its aspects."[11]

But whatever benefits this relational way of thinking has brought, it has too evidently not checked marital breakdown. On the contrary, divorce has proliferated, giving rise, surely, to more misery than happiness. So there has been a backlash. Relationships are regarded after all as "mere" relationships, liable to fluctuate and perish. "Some of us," said Dr. Graham Leonard, Bishop of London, "had traumatic evidence in our pastoral work of what happens when the existence of the marriage bond is made to rest upon the quality of the relationship."[12]

Many moralists feel that our "throw-away" society has gone too far and that personalism has let us down. In fairness it needs to be said that to be "reactionary" after this manner is not necessarily to be inhumane. People who believe in the permanence of marriage may be more optimistic about human nature than some liberals: they defend the idea that people are capable of making real, lasting commitments. What they are attacking is that kind of idolatry of relationships which seems to put any lasting bond at the mercy of immediate feelings.[13]

One does not have to be either a legalist or a rigorist to feel that "personal relationships" can be ambivalent and that some kinds of reliance upon them has over-reached itself. As Philip Turner has put it, "Vows which mean nothing more than, 'I will stay with you, as long as you are compatible and meet my needs,' mean little . . . [they] simply cannot provide marriage with a foundation the partners can count upon. The inevitable result is that relations between the sexes become increasingly tentative and increasingly experimental."[14]

So the pendulum swings back to a renewed emphasis upon the *institution* of marriage. It is being insisted afresh that marriage is more than relationship: it is a *state* persisting whether relationships hold firm or not. It is often called an "ontological" state for good measure.

The ensuing argument has been by no means free from confusion. It has been unhelpfully polarized into a straight-forward choice. Which *is* marriage, we seem to be asked, "given institution" *or* "personal relationship"? Invited in this way to take sides, rigorists plump for institution and liberals for relationship. Many people instinctively reply, "But it's both!"

and try to work out a compromise or strike a balance, a bit more institution and a bit less relationship, or vice versa. But we are not really dealing with ingredients of marriage like the ingredients in a pudding, more flour and less fat. The institution and the relationship belong to each other like form and content, structure and substance. We cannot have one without the other.

In any society, marriage is an institution. Two people take each other as husband and wife: they make vows before witnesses; they go through the forms required by law and custom; they are married. They take on legal and moral obligations from which they cannot extricate themselves without more legal processes, difficult or easy. People who believe in indissoluble marriage will say that they can never extricate themselves at all. But to find out what this bond is into which they have entered is to ask about its content as well as its form. There is no point in the insistence that marriage is a "state" without an indication of what sort of state, and to say what sort of state is to say something about what marriage is as relationship. This is not to get away from solid reality into a world of subjective feelings. Relationships, formal or informal, relaxed or difficult, pleasant or unpleasant, are not merely notional but are part of the world we all live in.

The "state of the question" appears to be that the rehabilitation of relationships has been successful up to a point: the point at which it begins to be felt to have gone too far. Christians cannot simply put their faith in personal relationships as the whole essence of the Gospel without more ado. Responsible moralists, looking at the world around us and repelled by the seemingly built-in obsolescence of fidelity among many of our contemporaries, are trying to recall us to a greater appreciation of the reality of the marriage bond. The permanence of marriage, they reiterate, is not something which may or may not develop, but is part of the very nature of marriage in God's eyes. In making vows to one another, human beings are doing something real and important. So we are invited to take sides in a way congenial to Christians, in favor of the objective rather than the subjective, and of real *union* rather than human changeableness.

It is tempting to feel that here we have come home, to the idea of *union* which surely sums up what marriage is. This is where we could too easily short-circuit the argument. This time the trouble is not that "union" points both ways, propitious and unpropitious. On the contrary, it is so propitious that both sides want it. But from the way the debate has happened to go, the rigorist side could too easily preempt "union" for itself. So we have to complicate the question by insisting that it belongs as naturally to the liberals.

The arguments of liberal and rigorist converge upon the idea of "union" from different directions. Both are concerned to reject any idea that marriage is a mere contract, though maybe their reasons for rejecting it are different. The rigorist concern is to stress permanent commitment rather than breakable arrangements; so rigorists will naturally lay claim to the concept of a real *union*. The liberal concern is to stress personal relationships; so liberals likewise need the concept of a union *of persons*, in contrast now to the impersonality of the legal contract. So each side in this dispute claims the right to base itself upon the biblical way of characterizing marriage, "they become one flesh." But there is scope for diverse variations upon this theme, and among the variations *personalism* remains very much alive.

At the center of all the discussion there are disagreements, both of terminology and of substance, about the slipperiest notion of them all, the notion of *person*, handy for commendation but not free from question-begging and confusion.[15] We use the word quite happily. If we think historically we are aware of the roots that the idea of a "person" has in the law, or in the theater: an autonomous being with rights and duties, or a "mask," a player of roles. We may be aware of various presuppositions and prejudices arising from this background. But most people, asked to define a "person," would be more inclined to point to plain examples of persons, ourselves and the other people around us. About these persons, two things are evident, both congenial to Christian faith: they are embodied and they are social. With these facts as data, Christians have plenty to say about creation, about love, and about sexuality. But they need to distinguish what they are assuming and what they are asserting.

We are all sure that "persons" matter and many of us believe that they matter supremely. So we warm to theories about human life which in one way or another say "up with persons." But "personalism," as generally understood, is not necessarily saying anything as uncontroversial as that. There is scope here for a head-on collision between two different ways of ascribing value to persons. The emphasis can be put, either upon their built-in *sacredness* (their intrinsic mattering, so to speak) or upon their *capacity for fulfillment* (what matters *to* them). Strange as it may seem, emphasis on the sacredness of persons goes with distrust of the theory called "personalism." This is because moralists who have claimed the name of personalist have concentrated so much upon fulfillment and developing value that the built-in value of persons has tended to disappear from view.

On the one hand, moral absolutists who believe that persons are intrinsically sacred take their stand on principle. They emphasize personal integrity and abhor utilitarian concessions to short-term satisfaction. Personal fulfillment is all very well but they are deeply suspicious of making it into a goal. Meanwhile, on the other hand, personalists have earmarked the idea of fulfillment. So they are more inclined to look favorably towards utilitarianism, because they cannot put aside the idea that sooner or later the happiness of persons is going to matter more than anything else. It is characteristic of personalists to be less convinced about absolute principles, and to find it hard to believe in laws of human nature which go against what people want to do.

Medical ethics is an area where the resulting conflicts are particularly sharp. There are clearcut arguments, especially about the beginning and end of life, about whether persons are inviolable at all costs, and what counts as a person. But sexual ethics, in a more confused way, becomes a battleground too. If persons matter supremely and human persons are sexual beings, what is the significance of sexual union, and to what duties does it give rise?

The arguments in medical and sexual ethics can run on parallel lines. In each the "personalist" concern with quality of life sounds wholly appropriate until it comes up against the sacredness of life. In medical ethics, moralists who care about absolutes are horrified by the notion that "quality of life" is allowed to become the criterion for value, so that helpless or handicapped human beings may be high-mindedly eliminated by abortion or euthanasia. Likewise in sexual ethics, absolutists are determined that human commitment shall not be put at the mercy of "quality of relationships."

Personalists tend to be less enthusiastic about absolutes such as the sacredness of life: such ideas, to them, seem too abstract for the realities of human existence, the miseries created for human beings by unbreakable principles. So personalists are more inclined to concentrate upon the capacity of persons to become happy or unhappy, their hopes and fears and aims and what they do to one another. Personalists sometimes believe that the end justifies the means, that a destructive state of affairs is better ended. When asked about the indissolubility of marriage or the sinfulness of living together unmarried, they say, "That depends." So however much Christians warm to personalism at the outset, they may well before long suffer a check. Instead of being obviously right and proper in its affirmation that people and their fulfillment is what matters, personalism can readily be portrayed unsympathetically as a soft and unprincipled moral theory.

Eventually a convincing personalist understanding will be more subtle, less mercenary, more reverent and more humane than its easily permissive caricature. But such an understanding can be developed only if proper account is taken of difficulties and objections. So if in trying to give a Christian account of the meaning of sexuality one is drawn towards personalism, one dares not treat such an approach as if it were self-evident. It needs definite deference.

Personalism Defended

The easiest objection to answer is the recurrent assumption that personalism is a capitulation to shallow expediency. There is no reason why the happiness that personalists value should be a short-term matter. On the contrary, a Christian personalist ought to be contented with nothing less than an eternal perspective. Quality of life here and now need not be the point at all. Austerity, even, is as live an option as permissiveness.

It is true that there has been a tendency for people who emphasize persons-in-relation to be flexible, some may well say too flexible, about what is to be done about impermanent relationships. Some people of liberal and humane intent, struggling against legalist and rigorist styles of upholding the unique sanctity of monogamous marriage, have seemed to be positively in favor of easy divorce, of unregulated liaisons and the pursuit of transient romance. But to go off on that tack is to abandon "persons-in-relation," not to uphold them. A more responsible personalism will go a long way with the argument characteristic of rigorists, that relationships need the expectation of permanence, need the support of firm, unwobbly frameworks and time and space to grow. It is not legalistic to talk about stability. A Christian personalist ought to be far from disagreeing with the value rigorists place on the known permanence of the married state, which, as Dr. Leonard put it, "sets a couple free to grow into the true personal relationship of marriage and delivers them from being at the mercy of their moods and difficulties."[16] As seriously, though less solemnly, Dr. Andrew Greeley asks, do children "play with strangers, casual acquaintances, people they don't care about?" The hedonists, he says "do not understand the dynamics or the phenomenology of play."[17] Robert Browning's lines are over-quoted but make the point:

> Grow old along with me
> The best is yet to be.

The glory of lifelong marriage is the time and security it can give for the development of relationship.

Where personalists do part company with rigorists is over the question of whether a bond can be real, strong and lasting without having the metaphysical property of "indissolubility." The attractiveness of rigorism is its certainty and the protection it offers against the thin ends of wedges, but its absoluteness is neither attractive nor wholly convincing. Personalists must dispense with such theoretical rigidity without going over into permissiveness. They have a difficult balance to maintain, but one that human beings badly need.

A more telling objection to personalism is that this way of regarding human life, brought in as a corrective to legalism, only too quickly develops a legalism of its own. The sequence is that liberal-minded Christians make common cause with humane skeptics on behalf of live human beings against dead metaphysics. But the freshness of the argument soon takes a negative turn. "It's not fair" to expect people to remain stuck in hopeless situations, or to be eternally faithful to the unfaithful because there is no way of setting them free. So legalism comes back into the argument by way of human rights and wrongs.

Almost without noticing it, this line of argument makes "persons" into right-bearers, who can be expected to do their duty but no more. Transcendent goodness quietly loses its grip and one settles down, still calling oneself a personalist, in a workaday morality of claims and counterclaims. There is a lot being written (partly argued, partly assumed) by philosophers nowadays about *respect for persons* as a moral principle, even as *the* moral principle.[18] This seems to chime in so well with Christian attitudes that one may overlook the haunting legalism which is apt to cling to it. Respect for persons is a matter for persons as bearers of rights; suddenly, with all goodwill, one is miles away from the generosity of spirit and self-abandonment which Christianity was meant to enable. Yet because "personalism" was embarked upon as an anti-legalistic view it is easy not to notice what is happening, or to feel no more than a vague dissatisfaction. One slips into a still legalistic and atomistic view of a world of separate individual persons with conflicting interests. Of course the hope is to harmonize these conflicts; but the very way the problem is posed seems to keep people apart rather than drawing them together.

It is this kind of "personalism" that Philip Turner has roundly repudiated, voicing a disquiet with the attitudes of some natural allies among our contemporaries. It is a disquiet that needed to be made explicit. The path from humanity via respect for persons to what he criticizes as "possessive individualism" is such a gentle slope that one may hardly realize how far one has come.[19] At first sight, if one has thought of oneself as a Christian personalist for many years, it seems exceedingly odd to find personalism blamed for excessive individualism. For it has been the relatedness of persons which has seemed to be the point of personalism, and the importance, even the ultimate importance, of personal relationship which has been the mainstay of its ethics. The argument is partly a matter of terminology, and partly a matter of emphasis; but it will not be properly resolved either my merely redefining one's terms or by merely taking sides. There are points being made on both hands which deserve the kind of consideration which puts away polemics.

Christian personalism is and ought to be uneasy with the slogan "respect for persons." If such a drearily legalistic formulation really sums up our morality, something is seriously lacking. Turner believes that personalism in this unsatisfactory sense has "a good chance of becoming the going Christian ethic of sex" and that among liberal clergy it may have "already carried the day." Against this tendency he sets the account in the first chapter of Genesis of the creation of Adam, that is, of humankind. "God said, 'Let us make man in our image, after our likeness'. . . . Male and female he created them." *Adam* is not a self-contained unit but a "social whole."[20]

Here the personalist, with all diffidence, comes back into the argument, claiming this understanding of the Genesis myth as a *personalist* understanding: persons-in-relation made in the image of God. What personalism at its most promising is feeling after is a profound concept: "unity-in-plurality." With a little patience, much more can be drawn out of the belief that persons matter more than is allowed by an atomistic individualism that respectfully isolates them from one another. There is a rich tradition here; once one looks, one finds this theme of unity *in* plurality repeating itself throughout Christian teaching. From the doctrine of the Trinity in heaven to the marriage bond on earth one can recognize built into the structure of reality, forms of union which do not swallow up or confound the persons entering into them but even enhance their distinctiveness. Human beings are not, as it were, like gingerbread men stamped out, made individual by what divides them from one another, or like billiard balls pushing each other about. We can see for ourselves that people find themselves and develop as the valuable and sacred creatures that they are in essential relationship to one another: to parents, first of all, to siblings, friends, and neighbors—and, most important for the present discussion, in relation to spouses. We shape one another's lives, like trees planted near together; but more than that, we need one another to be ourselves.

What "personalism," carefully explained, can do for Christians is pick up their basic hold-all concept of *love* and fill it in realistically and humanly as what people need. The love which "makes the world go round" is not a luxury, making life more agreeable for us as separate units, but the warmth and nourishment we require to keep us human. So a personalist sexual ethic need not say permissively, "Do as you want," or, legalistically, "Respect persons," as if either of these summed up morality. It will say something much more like, "It is not good that human beings should be alone."

It is at this promising stage that personalism is beset by the more insidious error of proving too much. The union between a man and a woman is such a satisfactory example of the recurring Christian theme of unity-in-plurality that it is a standing temptation to let it assume a disproportionate theological significance.

When metaphysics and common sense speak with one voice it is no wonder that we are impressed. Metaphysics tells us that marriage is an indissoluble bond, which may or may not seem plain. Meantime we know what it means in everyday life to say that husband and wife become one, legally and morally, yet without submerging their distinct identities. Is that not the kind of thing Christians want to affirm, more obscurely, about the Trinity or the Communion of Saints? We can use the familiar to illuminate the unfamiliar, in real encouragement.

But to go on from here to talk about marriage as if it were the *same thing* as the Communion of Saints and the only true meaning of the image of God in humankind is theologically inadequate and practically dangerous. Christian love is not all summed up in finding a mate. There is a potential tyranny of the conventional "couple" which can be bitterly cruel to unmarried people and to unhappily married people. Now that Christians are less inclined to belittle marriage in favor of celibacy, they are more inclined to become sentimentally idealistic about the married state. Nor does it help when, trying to be tolerant and realistic, they confine their idealism to something called "Christian marriage," not seeming to care if they leave everyone else, whether responsible and faithful or quite otherwise, out in the cold.

Unless Christian moralists are to set in motion an unhappy see-saw of well-meaning assertions, rebellious denials and reassertions, they must sort out what they really want to say about the theology of marriage. A good deal of the present discussion goes back, whether the participants recognize this or not, to Karl Barth.[21] What he says about marriage is potentially of great interest to personalists, although, or perhaps because, he is in a way a prize example of proving too much.[22] His theology is much more positive and even inspiring than the caricatures which are too easily made of it. It starts so many constructive and formative trains of thought that it is worth exploring both hopefully and critically. To criticize him summarily for slipping over a knife edge is to lose the chance of following him in some exciting territory near it.

It has to be admitted that there are aspects of Barth's thought which will repel liberal-minded Christians, not as proving too much, but as *wrong*: in particular his determination to uphold the superiority of man over woman. But to treat this as the whole story would be heavy-handed.

Barth's great point is that God is not "a lonely God." This is what he draws from "Let us make man in our image," not in

any pedestrian liberalist spirit but in the light of Christian belief
in God as Trinity. "Man is the repetition of this divine form of
life; its copy and reflection" and that is why "it is not good that
the man should be alone. . . . because solitary man would not
be man created in the image of God, who Himself is not
solitary."[23]

From this, much follows. It would be a great pity if this
enlightenment had to be limited to the theology of marriage.
The risk that Barth does not always avoid is to imply "that *only*
in marriage . . . . does a person become fully human." [24]

From Barth's whole magisterial exposition we can seize on
two main ideas about humankind, each of which the Christian
tradition has sometimes seemed to lose: the essential interrelatedness of human beings and their fundamentally bodily
character. When these ideas are combined we can indeed apply
them to sexual morality and appreciate the "proper meaning
and seriousness of the sexual relation as such." We can get rid
of the abstractness which has beset a good deal of Christian
sexual teaching, and talk, as Barth does, about reality. For
instance, he is excellently scornful about the stereotyping of
man and woman: "Thou shalt be concerned with things
(preferably machines) and thou with persons! Thou shalt
cherish the mind, thou the soul! Thou shalt follow thy reason
and thou thy instinct! Thou shalt be objective and thou subjective! Thou shalt build and thou merely adorn; thou shalt con-
quer and thou cherish!"[25]

Of all theologians, Barth cannot be appreciated in other
people's accounts of his thought. It has to be sampled directly.
His exegesis of the creation stories and of the Song of Songs
gets away from the besetting tendency of Christian sexual
ethics, its over-emphasis on procreation as the sole justification

for sexual relationships. He restores to us the conviction that marriage has its own validity and is able to be "a sign and symbol representing fellowship between God and man."[26] Human life as we find it and theology as we learn it shed light upon one another—as we should expect if human life is indeed God's creation. Human beings are made for unity-in-plurality, and marriage is an excellent example of this.

What we do not have to do is make marriage more than an example, the very nature of unity-in-plurality. We do not have to put together the interrelatedness of human beings and their bodiliness in such a way as to allow sexual ethics to take over the whole theology of creation. It is admirable to recognize "the radical, sexual duality" of humanity, but it is overdoing it to assert, as Barth does at one point, that this is "at the root of all other fellowship." Unfortunately this overemphasis has been heeded, in admiration or in disagreement, as if an account of sexuality could be a complete account of humankind made in the image of God. He puts the matter less misleadingly when he maintains that "humanity . . . is in its root fellow-humanity." Barth himself gives quite as telling a warning as his critics against the danger of proving too much. He commends the analogy in Ephesians between the marriage bond and the unity of Christ and the church, and promptly points out that if the two ideas which are being used to illuminate each other were identical we simply would have no analogy. If "analogy becomes identity" there is nothing to compare. He adds, "This exaltation of marriage is dearly bought."[27]

It is easy to slip from illuminating exegesis into an exaggeration which destroys the point. From Barth's interpretation of the creation stories we have seized the idea that human beings as relational creatures are made for unity-in-plurality and marriage illustrates this. If we slip into saying that human beings as sexual creatures are made for marriage, we have both overstated the case about the meaning of marriage and lost our theological illumination. Such an exaltation of marriage is indeed dearly bought, inadequate in theory and potentially cruel in practice.

Two-Way Illumination

Yet what understanding of marriage would not be dearly bought? When we have indicated that a personalistic view need not be permissive, taken heed of the tendency of personalism to become in its turn legalistic, and then refused to let this relational ethic of sex quietly colonize the whole of ethics, at what positive illumination have we arrived? The object of this exercise has been to claim that marriage, as the *union* of a man and a woman in its human reality, characteristically exemplifies a theme which runs through Christian theology, the theme of *personal immanence.*

The claim is double. First, the notion of a unity that is compatible with distinctness sums up so effectively what marriage aspires to be that it is an illuminating way of describing the reality we know. Next, the illumination goes both ways, because marriage as familiar reality can shed light on what "personal immanence" can mean as a theological idea.[28]

Once one looks, one finds this theme of unity in plurality cropping up all over Christian theology. It can seem baffling and even contradictory. How can God be Three and One? How can Christ be in us and we in him? How can he suffer for us? How can divine grace not swamp the human will? The twoness and oneness of husband and wife, their independence and interdependence, their acting for one another, can illuminate these strange and demanding dogmas by showing how they make sense in earthly reality. Marriage can signify "the mystical union that is betwixt Christ and his Church" not because it is itself a mystical union, but on the contrary because it is human and familiar. It is as a thoroughly secular reality existing in its own right that marriage can be "a useful finite model of divine realities."[29]

This is the moment to go back, not legalistically but prosaically, to the legal definition. In English law marriage is "the union of one man with one woman, voluntarily entered into for life," and here precisely is the notion of unity-in-plurality. It is legally, not just poetically, that a married couple may be treated for some purposes as one person. They are evidently in some senses still two entities: there is no confusion here, but they are not two separate entities, either. Their association has a reality such that even in the eyes of the law the whole is greater than the sum of its parts. It is not an ordinary contract which may be brought to an end at the mere will of the parties, but a "contract conferring status" which requires the intervention of a court for its dissolution.[30]

Nor are these aspects of marriage legal fictions. They correspond to common-sense realities. Make all needful allowance for human diversity and it still remains true that, in society as we know it, it is an entirely ordinary state of affairs for the bond between husband and wife to enhance, not destroy, their individuality. "Dependence" and "independence" are necessary ways of characterizing their relationship, and something like the terminology of grace and freedom can be used quite readily without the anxious logic-chopping which has sometimes characterized its more theological applications. One finds it natural, not baffling, that a husband and wife should feel that they need each other to be fully themselves, and that they should be wholly unable to sort out mathematically what is of one, what is of the other, and what is of both. Whatever they feel for one another, their lives are joined by a common concern which makes the word "union" an accurate characterization of a way of life, not a half-dead cliche).

This way of characterizing marriage as *union* can gather up the ideas of *partnership, covenant* and *relationship* in a *personalist* account which need not be permissive or legalistic. But does it still overreach itself? So far, most of what has been said about the unity-in-plurality of married people could be said just as well about friendship. This is hardly surprising, because a good marriage develops either from friendship or into friendship. But the rather surprising risk arises now that this version of personalism will lose touch with, or be muddled about, the essentially *embodied* character of the marriage union.

Friendship, it needs to be said, need have very little to do with union. It hopes for permanence but not for exclusiveness. So a sexual ethic that bases itself, thoroughly humanely, upon friendship, and then tries to make sex fit in, is apt disconcertingly to find that "forsaking all others" has become an optional extra or even a possessive aberration; marriage becomes a "mystery" in quite the wrong sense.

People today are apt to feel fairly safe from the prudish other-worldliness that tries to leave out sex altogether. The greater likelihood now is that sexuality takes on a life of its own without finding its meaning in union. There is one kind of "personalism" that starts promisingly with a high view of friendship and a realistic acknowledgment of human embodiment, but then tries to combine these in an almost happy-go-lucky way. The assumption is that because we are embodied creatures any close relationship must be or become a sexual relationship. Here we have two persons-in-relations: should they not give physical expression to their affection even if it turns out to be temporary or even if they are of the same gender?[31] So, by beginning with friendship and then adding in sex, we arrive at a high-minded do-as-you-please permissiveness out of which it is hard to escape except through various kinds of legalistic prohibition.

Unless marriage is the uniting of two lives, it will seem to be no more than the licensing of a particular kind of pleasure; it is bound to seem arbitrary to grant this license only in such exclusive forms. But when the union of a man and a woman is treated as fundamental, exclusiveness comes into its own as part of the meaning of union. Whether people "make friends" first and then "fall in love," or fall in love first and then make friends, or abide by the choice of their elders, or even enter into a marriage of convenience, the meaning of marriage is that they take each other for life as husband and wife. Their physical unity is not something to be added into the account as an extra. "One flesh" is the basis, however much we want as personalists to enrich this notion with emphasis on relationship.

We can now try to reckon with one more slippery term, the notion of *sacrament*. Sacramental theology has often been applied to marriage in confusing ways. St. Paul's "great mystery" has been taken up and used rigidly and even tyrannically. The mystical union between Christ and the church has been fastened upon the human bond of marriage like a straitjacket rather than a means of grace.

But the particular point of a sacrament is not that it is mystical, still less ecclesiastical, but that it is physical. An earthly reality makes spiritual reality findable. The water of baptism, the bread and wine of the Eucharist, and, we may well say, the union of husband and wife, are capable of having meaning beyond themselves. A *means* of grace is just that: a vehicle or carrier of grace, a way by which grace becomes embodied.[32] The persistent legalism of Western Christianity has frequently obscured this. Are there strictly two sacraments or seven? Surely there *can* be hundreds, and it is hardly for us to be possessively sure which are "necessary for salvation." For many people, not all Christians, their marriages in their earthly reality are vivid signs of the meaning of grace.

One way of expressing the sacramental character of marriage is to say that husband and wife as ministers of this sacrament actually convey God's grace to one another. It would be, precisely, ungracious to underestimate this way of looking at it. But a more complicated approach may be more accessible to the less devout. What we have been saying is that the unity-in-plurality of marriage, the one-flesh union, is the most ordinary and clearest *model* we have of the *meaning* of divine grace. So the emphasis is put on understanding our hopes, not on making instant claims for which many of us are not ready. The reason for the sacramental language is to make plain that the physical basis of the marriage union is not just theologically acceptable, it is positively fit to be the foundation of the two-way illumination we have been searching after.

SEXUAL ETHICS AND THE SINGLE LIFE

Victor Preller, O.G.S.

I

Both of the expressions used in the title of this chapter, "sexual ethics" and "the single life," are quite modern. They are themselves symptomatic of the very aspects of contemporary culture that have occasioned the debate to which this chapter is a response. Formerly one would have looked in vain for separate ethical treatises on the "sexual" aspects of life. That sex is now regarded as a subject deserving of independent treatment is a function of complex changes in our way of thinking about the dynamics of human behavior and about human nature itself.

In our culture, the dominant model of human nature is oddly individualistic and naturalistic: human nature is seen to operate in an individual independently of society and culture. The basic determinants of human behavior are those cravings or desires (such as hunger, thirst, curiosity, or sexual passion) that we naturally experience as psycho-biological individuals. The only goods by which we are naturally motivated are those things that satisfy our natural cravings or desires, and the goods to which we are ordered by our experience of sexual passion internal to sexual activity itself: sexual gratification and pleasure. Our orientation to those goods is determined by nature, prior to any social or cultural considerations. They are naturally and universally experienced as motivating goods. While sexual activity may terminate in the procreation of offspring, that end is not naturally or universally experienced as a motivating good. The desire for offspring as an *external* good of sexual activity is optional and acquired—it is a matter of taste or choice.

Social institutions, such as marriage, and the goods or ends defined by them, are viewed as conventional additions to human nature. It is "natural" that a man might seek to gratify his sexual passions and desires. It is merely "conventional" that in certain societies he might decide to marry. The single life is therefore an extension of a man's or a woman's "natural" state. To marry is to introduce the "conventional" into one's definition of goods to be pursued.

The "sexual revolution" that has radically changed the attitudes and behavior of many members of our society—especially of the young and the single—is simply a matter of putting into practice the individualistic and naturalistic model of human nature that has been with us since the eighteenth and nineteenth centuries. Almost every contemporary deviation from "traditional sexual ethics" can be explained by reference to that model. The terms in which the supporters of the sexual revolution explain and justify their behavior are either drawn from it or are natural extensions of it.

Accordingly, sexual gratification and sexual pleasure are natural goods in and of themselves. While the procreation of offspring is a natural consequence of sexual intercourse, it is not by nature included among the goods we intentionally pursue. The intention to have children is radically separable from the intention to pursue the goods internal to sexual intercourse. Now that we have the necessary contraceptive and abortive technology, it is possible to exclude offspring from the consequences of sexual activity as well. The natural desire to gratify our sexual passions is more basic to our human nature than any social or cultural conventions having to do with marriage and family. Men and women are by nature oriented to sex; they are not by nature oriented to marriage. They may naturally (and thus rationally and ethically) pursue the natural goods internal to sexual activity whether or not they choose to pursue the conventional (and thus optional) social good of marriage. Since sexual intercourse is naturally or physiologically ordered to the procreation of offspring, a decision to pursue that external good is a natural option that is more basic than any social conventions concerning marriage and family structure. Nature and culture (the residue of social conventions) are radically distinguished, and nature provides us with our fundamental ethical justifications. Since we are justified by nature in our pursuit of natural goods, the pursuit of those goods is a "natural right" that cannot be abrogated by mere social convention. Thus individuals have a natural right to seek sexual gratification and, when desired, children, apart from any secondary social conventions such as marriage.

It seems quite clear that the arguments and justifications offered by defenders of the "sexual revolution" are completely consistent with what is surely the dominant model of human nature in our culture. The ethical concepts that they deploy seem, indeed, to presuppose such a model. Arguments and justifications—the very terms and concepts—used by traditional moralists are radically discontinuous with such a model. What could possibly be made of such traditional terms as "temperance" and "chastity" in the context of such a naturalistic and individualistic view of human nature? Hence it is not surprising that for the modern world such terms have lost their original meaning, and seem quaint, old-fashioned, arbitrary, or downright silly.

It is not simply that some goods that traditional moralists say we ought to pursue are relegated by modern ethicists to the realm of the conventional and thus of the optional. It is rather that the grounds on which traditional moralists argue that we ought to pursue such goods presuppose that human nature is social through and through—that there are no "natural goods" in the modern sense. All ethical justification makes reference to the "common good" of men and women in society. For a traditional moral theologian like Aquinas, for example, the natural (and thus rational) ends of sexual intercourse are not sexual gratification and pleasure, but rather *commixtio maris et feminae et educatio liberorum*—the merging of a man and a woman and the education of their offspring. Sexual gratification and pleasure are goods to be enjoyed, but only as they are ordered to the pursuit of goods external to the sexual act itself—the unity of husband and wife, the procreation and education of children, and the stability of the social order.

Nor, for the traditional moralist, are there any "natural rights" in the modern sense. What we have a "right" to do at any time is a function of the demands of justice—and the demands of justice are ordered to the "common good" of all of the members of our community. Rights accrue to individuals as they pursue in common with their fellow men and women a just and peaceful society. By nature (by our truly human nature) we are ordered to the acquisition of such virtuous dispositions of character as are appropriate to our status as social beings in the simultaneous pursuit of our own good and the good of our fellow citizens.

We are ordered *by nature* to social goods and to social roles, which are therefore neither merely conventional nor arbitrary. All rationally motivated human action is ordered to a social good and performed in the context of a way of life that is defined by a social role. There is no such thing as living in accord with a pre-social or pre-cultural human nature. Thus the single life is not an extension of the natural state of men and women, but a culturally defined way of life that is rationally and ethically justified by its orientation to social goods—by its contribution to the "common good." It is neither more nor less "conventional" than marriage.

If the individualistic and naturalistic model of human nature is correct—if it provides an authoritative account of the goods to which we are ordered by nature itself—then the central concepts of traditional sexual ethics (and the arguments and justifications within which they are deployed) have lost their meaning. They do not apply to the real world, and therefore they should be abandoned.

Many members of the church, including a significant number of priests and bishops, apparently believe that that is the case. They speak knowingly of our "new scientific knowledge" of human sexuality, knowledge that calls our traditional sexual ethics into radical question. Assuming that the eighteenth- and nineteenth-century model of an individualistic and naturalistic human nature represents the latest findings of the scientific community, they are willing to adopt it as a model for human behavior. Finding themselves theoretically in accord with the defenders of the sexual revolution, they are calling for a fairly drastic revision of the church's attitudes and teachings concerning sexuality.

Many of the more controversial proposals of the new reformers have to do with the sexual activities and parental status of the single—those who are unmarried, divorced, or widowed. We are told that "new realities" in our culture call for a new openness to alternative modes of sexual relationships and family structure. The church is sometimes called upon to give its institutional blessing to "committed couples" who wish to live together and to share a full sexual life outside the bonds of matrimony. The proviso is sometimes added that such unmarried couples should promise (on social grounds) not to have children. Thus the church is asked to bless sexual acts while mandating the exclusion from those acts of the good of procreation. In any case, it would seem that "committed" means something like "committed so long as we both shall desire," which would strike some members of the church as an odd sort of commitment indeed. Some of the new reformers have suggested that the church provide a liturgy for the blessing of "homosexual marriages." The fact that the phrase "homosexual marriage" does not strike them as oxymoronic would seem to indicate that they have a different understanding of marriage from those who support the traditional teachings of the church.

A well-known bishop recently commended an unmarried priest who had a child by inseminating herself with semen left in her apartment (after discrete acts of masturbation) by four male friends. The bishop spoke of her actions as a worthy and courageous attempt to define an alternative form of "family life." In an interview carried on national television, he challenged dissident viewers to cite any biblical commandment that the priest had broken. And, of course, the movement to legitimate the ordination of self-proclaimed and practicing homosexuals is maintaining, if not gaining, momentum. No wonder that there is much puzzlement and head-shaking amongst traditional members of the church.

Many of the new reformers would be somewhat upset that I have associated their proposals with the ethics of the sexual revolution. After all, they might say, we still hold to the traditional Christian belief that the ideal expression of sexuality is within the context of a committed, lifelong, marital relationship. We are simply saying that alternative forms of sexual relations are also justified under certain circumstances, however they might fall short of the Christian ideal. While not ordered to or productive of as much human good as is marital sex, so the argument runs, they are nonetheless directed to real natural goods. It would therefore be arbitrary and irrational to forbid them across the board, or to declare them intrinsically immoral.

The problem with such a reply lies in its argument that these alternative forms of sexual relations are ordered to real natural goods, and are *therefore* rational and ethically justified. This argument cannot be supported without reference to something like the individualistic and naturalistic model of human nature that we have been considering. It needs, I believe, the distinction between the "natural" and the "conventional." It simply adds a further distinction between the "natural" and the "theologically ideal." Once again, if the individualistic and naturalistic model of human nature is correct, then the new reformers are right, and traditional sexual ethics must be abandoned—and along with it, the traditional teaching of the church.

I believe that there are good reasons to reject the demands of the new reformers and to defend the traditional teaching of the church concerning human sexuality. Those reasons, I believe, are biblical, theological, and social. I am not convinced, however, that they have been very well articulated by the most vocal and public critics of the new reformers. The grounds on which the church has traditionally refused to affirm or sanction the full expression of sexual powers and passions outside of a lifelong commitment to marital fidelity between a man and a woman are obscured and rendered arbitrary when they are encapsulated in summary epithets wielded as weapons of war against the forces of evil. The very intention of the church—a loving and caring concern for the true good of men and women—is distorted when its representatives can find nothing more to say about contemporary deviations from traditional sexual norms than that they are "immoral," "unacceptable," "wrong," "evil," "abominable," or even "unbiblical." They may indeed be some or all of those things. But the simple repetition of biblical passages or traditional moral conclusions is no substitute for conversation, argument, and persuasion.

No number of proof texts cited from Scripture is sufficient to warrant a particular moral judgment when the very reading or interpretation of the relevant texts is precisely what is at issue. When men and women are addressed in Scripture by the Word of God, they are addressed as creatures of God immersed in the contingencies of history. How we read or interpret a particular text—how we hear and obey the Word of God—is in part a function of our cultural and historical situatedness. God can no more speak to our intellects apart from that situatedness than he can create a square circle. That is why, for Anglicans, Scripture requires for its interpretation a reference to historical tradition. It is our situatedness within the living tradition of the historical church that must primarily inform our hearing and obeying of the Word of God. The traditional teachings of the church (in all of their historical contingency and complexity) are the distillation of the Word of God as heard through the years by the people of God. To deny their authority is to deny our history and our culture. It is to become theological solipsists.

While the very existence of a tradition of moral teaching within the church is in and of itself a good reason for being chary about its abandonment in any particular instance, it is still true that the tradition of Christian moral teaching has in fact been reformed in particular instances—the relatively recent condemnation of slavery is a good example—and in all justice and charity it may have to be reformed in other particular instances in the future. Furthermore, a tradition of moral teaching is no more self-interpreting than is Scripture itself. The application of moral precepts to individual cases requires interpretation. The more radical the changes in historical and cultural circumstances, the more difficult it becomes to depend on tradition to interpret tradition. The exclusion of interest charged for borrowed money from the prohibition of usury is an instance of the creative interpretation of traditional Christian moral teaching in the light of new historical and cultural circumstances. In the process of that interpretation, moral concepts were redefined and applied in novel ways. There is no guarantee that changing historical and cultural circumstances may not again require—in all justice and charity—the redefinition and novel application of traditional moral concepts. That is why, for Anglicans, reason has its role to play in the faithful hearing of the Word of God within the historical situatedness of tradition. And that is why a "fortress mentality" that forecloses conversation, argument, and persuasion by an appeal to biblical fundamentalism or traditional literalism is wrong. It is unreasonable and therefore untheological. It stands in heretical opposition to the doctrine of creation. It is the methodology of sectarianism.

On the other hand, while human reason in its created nature is a rather humble thing, it has a tendency to become proud. If the rejection of reason in the name of tradition is heretical, so also is the rejection of tradition in the name of reason. It is not only heretical, it is also unreasonable. Reason is untrue to its created nature if it attempts to surmount its own historicality. Reasoning begins with what it has received. As Aristotle says, "All learning makes use in whole or in part of what we already know." It takes its start from the authority of tradition, and it proceeds by means of conversation. (That is true not only of theological or moral reasoning, but of all reasoning.) Reasonable moral conversation is rooted in tradition, and open to the possibility that changes in historical and cultural circumstances may require an interpretive redefinition and a novel application of traditional moral concepts. For the Christian, however, any departure from a traditional interpretation of Scripture must take the form of a better interpretation of Scripture. The burden of proof lies on the new reformers, who must persuade their fellow Christians that the Word of God must now be heard and obeyed in novel ways—if it is to be heard at all.

If, however, the burden of proof lies on the new reformers, the burden of listening lies on all in equal portion. The refusal to listen is tantamount to excommunication. And excommunication, whether pronounced by the church or by an individual, must surely be, like exorcism, a last resort. The history of the church should warn us that premature excommunication is more likely to lead to schism and sectarianism than to the purification of the Body of Christ. Much of the history of Christian theology has been concerned with recovering the truth that lies hidden within positions that were once declared anathema—the truth that orthodox members of the church were at that time unable to hear. The first response of the defenders of tradition to the new reformers must surely be to listen for the truth in what they say. Then the conversation may begin in earnest.

II

Those who would have us radically reform our notions of sexual ethics, and thus of the goods to which sexual acts are ordered, are often able to point to real evils that have resulted from the imposition of the traditional moral teachings of the church. Among the evils often cited are the feelings of guilt and shame that traditional modes of ethical teaching seem to produce—especially among the young. It must be granted, I believe, that the new reformers have a point. But it is a point that requires us to make some careful distinctions. I take it that no serious Christian ethicist would be satisfied with a mode of ethical teaching that *terminates* in the production of feelings of guilt and shame—in the young or in the old. If the reformers mean to imply, however, that feelings of guilt and shame are always a bad thing—that moral teachings must be so tailored to the human psyche that they never bring about such dysfunctional and potentially destructive feelings—then they are simply mistaken. A conscious recognition of guilt and a feeling of shame are part and parcel of moral maturation. Would that the defenders of apartheid recognized their guilt and experienced the shame appropriate to their unjust and inhumane behavior!

And yet there is a valuable insight underlying the new reformers' dismay at the "feelings of guilt and shame" that have often been the sole or the dominant result of subjection to certain unfortunate articulations of the traditional Christian understanding of human sexuality. We might say that the sort of guilt and shame that has often been associated with imperfect or disordered sexual activity, and which is even regarded by some moralizers as a desirable end of moral education, has more to do with the non-moral categories of "purity" and "defilement" than with the moral categories of "virtue" and "vice." Terms such as "dirty," "filthy," and "polluted" are applied both to the illicit sexual activity itself and to those who indulge in it. The language of defilement tends to carry with it not only a total rejection of the activity itself as wholly evil and "abominable," but also an excommunication of the agent from the society of those to whom love and respect are due. The person who engages in such activities is stigmatized as "contaminated" and thus unacceptable and unlovable as a person. The feelings of guilt and shame experienced by those who have been made to feel "dirty" are not the product of a proper moral evaluation of the goods and ends of human sexuality, but of the sort of non-rational fear and loathing directed in some primitive societies to lepers and other "abominations."

Those who speak of homosexuality, for example, as an abomination are associating it—in biblical terms—with leprosy, menstruation, and four-legged beasts that do not chew the cud! It "defiles" because it is categorically "impure" and thus "dirty." The major ground of condemnation is culturally acquired abhorrence of anomaly and fear of contamination. Such non-rational characterizations of homosexual activities and agents has no place, I should claim, in Christian morality. It is sad to think of parents whose notion of sexual education is to characterize the inchoate adolescent sexual fumblings of their children as "dirty" or "abominable." It is even sadder to think of self-proclaimed Christians (and even priests) who characterize homosexuals as "queers," or who treat them as moral lepers who have forfeited all claim to Christian love and social concern. The devastating effects that they have had on the souls and spirits of human beings is incalculable. Their own sins against justice and charity doubtless outweigh the perceived moral defects of those whom they loath and ostracize. We are indebted to the new reformers for recalling our attention to the primacy of charity in Christian ethics.

There are, of course, more subtle forms of the ethics of purity and defilement. Among them is a categorical distinction between "morality" and "immorality." Our current moral vocabulary encourages us to distinguish between those acts (or classes of acts) that are moral and those that are immoral. It is "moral" to kiss one's wife; it is "immoral" to have sex with someone who is not one's wife. While I do not claim a privileged status for the moral vocabulary of St. Thomas Aquinas, it should nonetheless provide food for thought that he never made use of such a distinction. It was not available to him. The characterization of actions or classes of actions as either moral or immoral is peculiarly modern, for these notions simply did not exist prior to the modern period. To characterize some action or pattern of behavior as either one or the other is to paint with too wide a brush.

It is no wonder that the Standing Commission on Human Affairs and Health of the Episcopal Church, in its 1988 report to the General Convention, found it necessary to couch most of its conclusions in such tentative language. The members of the Commission were clearly loath to categorize certain sorts of human acts or relationships in terms of the black-or-white terminology that they had available to them. It is saying both too much and too little to label premarital sex, for example, as "immoral"—and be done with it. While certain instances of tentative judgments may have been due to deep-seated disagreements among members of the Commission, it is also highly likely that many of the disagreements reflect the lack of a sufficiently nuanced moral vocabulary. Consequently they had no way of providing an account of "less than ideal" sexual acts or relationships that would still pay due respect to the positive or potentially redemptive aspects of those acts or relationships that the "liberals" did not wish to see denied, while defining in more precise terms the factors that make them morally unacceptable to the "traditionalists."

Yet another variation on the ethics of purity and defilement are certain versions of "divine command ethics." In its pure form it is rightly rejected by the new reformers as both fundamentalist and irrational. The pure form of divine command ethics was formulated by the scholastic followers of Ockham. In a misguided attempt to affirm the creative freedom of God against the emanationist theories of the neo-Averroists, Ockham claimed that God's decision to create the kind of world that he did create was based on a completely arbitrary act of will. That means that God was not constrained by any pre-existent standards of good and evil. He did not order creation as he did because he knew that such an order would be good by some standard other than his own free and arbitrary act of will. Rather, the order that he created is good because he freely and arbitrary decided to create it in the way that he did.

Similarly, the acts that God commands human beings to perform are good simply because God commands them. He does not command them because they are intrinsically or naturally good—participations or reflections, for example, of the natural goodness of God himself. In his most extreme rhetorical moods, Ockham says that God might just as well have commanded the opposite of what he does in fact command; and then those *commanded* acts (such as random murder or hatred for God) would be good in exactly the same sense in which the acts that he has actually commanded (such as love for one's neighbor) are good! We are ethically bound to act in any particular way only because God arbitrarily wills and commands such acts. The irony is that Ockham's view of the arbitrary will of God, while intended as a defence against neo-Averroism, is more Islamic than Christian!

We might ascribe Ockham's extreme rhetoric to an imperfect grasp of counter-factual logic. But, by the time his teachings had reached Martin Luther, they were taken absolutely literally. Luther, in his pre-Reformation *Lectures on Romans*, took Ockham's divine command ethics one step further. He claimed that, because of original sin, God hates all human acts. In their intrinsic nature as human acts, they are so permeated by sin that they deserve damnation even if they are in accord with what God commands. Viewed in their intrinsic nature as human acts, all of Christ's own works—including his mounting of the cross—deserved damnation! God, however, freely and arbitrary decided to regard the human acts of Christ as righteous and as the source of all redemption from sin. (Thus, the resurrection.) Merely acting in accord with God's arbitrary commands does not make our actions good. Only faith in the redeeming power of Christ will make our acts acceptable to God, through a free and arbitrary act of his will. Thus only God's free and arbitrary will can make our acts *good*—not naturally or intrinsically good, but good by imputation. The standard Protestant appropriation of Luther's divine command ethics involves a slight variation. Merely acting in accord with God's commands is not sufficient to render our acts good or acceptable. Only when we act out of sheer obedience to what God commands are our acts acceptable to him, and in that sense "good."

Certainly any Christian must say that whatever God commands is good and must be done. The commandments of God are to be obeyed. The fact that God commands an act constitutes a good reason—for Christians, the best possible reason—for performing that act. However, for a commandment to constitute a good reason for performing an act, the one to whom the commandment is issued must have a prior and independent relationship with the one who commands, a relationship that makes it just and reasonable to follow his commands. Christians obey what they take to be the commandments of God because they believe that God is good, that he wills our good, and that what he commands is intrinsically and really good. We have reason to believe that God commands what he does because it is good. It is not good simply because he commands it.

A pure rhetoric of obedience, like that of certain evangelical Protestants, can have no other foundation or justification than an extreme form of divine command ethics. It contradicts the traditional Christian doctrine of creation, which holds that whatever God creates is really, intrinsically, and naturally good. When Christian traditionalists respond to certain sexual acts by simply quoting proof-texts from Scripture, and characterizing those acts as disobedience to the commandments of God, the new reformers may rightly suspect that the ground of the condemnation is fundamentalist and irrational; they are perfectly justified in demanding a thicker description of the matter. Unless proponents of the traditional ethics of sex are able to provide more illuminating moral descriptions than "It's immoral," or "It's disobedient," ethical discussion is likely to end in nothing but moralistic footstamping on both sides.

The problem is that our contemporary moral vocabulary is so impoverished that there are no commonly accepted criteria for a nuanced analysis of human actions in morally relevant terms. We have become very good at analyzing human actions in purely naturalistic or physical terms—placing them, as Aquinas would say, in their "natural genus." We are able to discuss in excruciating detail the physiological and psychological determinants of human behavior, and the impact of certain sorts of actions or abstentions on an individual's physiological or psychological health. Of course such analyses are not irrelevant to ethical judgments, but unless the individualistic and naturalistic model of human nature is to be accepted, such analyses are not sufficient for a properly moral evaluation. Moral integrity is not the same thing as physical or mental health, although some of the new reformers seem to argue as though it were. Unless we are simply to turn all questions of morality over to the physicians and psychologists, we need to recover something of the richness of traditional moral analyses of human acts.

The moral vocabulary of Thomas Aquinas surely has the authority of long usage and widespread acceptance. It deeply influenced the writings of such classical Anglican moralists as Hooker and Taylor. That, of course, does not make it the only, or necessarily the best vocabulary in terms of which to analyze human actions. It has, however, two advantages. First, the complexity of its analysis of human action allows for nuanced moral judgments that do more than characterize actions as moral or immoral, good or bad, virtuous or vicious. Second, its mode of analysis, derived largely from Aristotle, is pragmatically based on the sorts of questions that we tend to ask when we attempt to understand an action and its moral implications: "What exactly did he do? Why did he do it? What means did he use? What were the consequences?" etcetera. (There is often more moral wisdom in the everyday questions posed by ordinary people than in the theoretical categories of philosophers and ethicists.)

Nonetheless, simply repeating the analytic vocabulary of Aquinas is likely to have little more than antiquarian interest. It must be shown that it can contribute to the clarification of contemporary ethical conversation and argument. I shall therefore try to deploy that vocabulary in the context of pursuing a conversation with the new reformers, listening always for the truth in what they say. By doing so, it may be possible to identify areas of unexpected agreement, as well as to locate more precisely the points at which we disagree.

III

One of the most telling criticisms addressed to traditionalists by the new reformers is that their black-or-white condemnations of "less than ideal" sexual behavior fails to recognize the good, praiseworthy, or potentially redemptive dimensions of that behavior. How might Aquinas respond to that criticism?

His first response would be radically theological: "Insofar as anything has being, it is good." The good of creation cannot be destroyed by the disordered, finite will of human beings. There is no such thing as a perfectly evil act. There cannot be. (Think of the eternal frustration of Satan!) The absolute absence of good is the absolute absence of being. At the heart of every human act, however sinful, vicious, or disordered, there is a ground of created good that God holds firmly in existence—a good that must be loved with the unremitting love of charity. That ground of created good constitutes the powers of the soul itself: it is what we mean by "person." And so the sinner must be loved, really loved. Any thought, word, or deed that expresses anything less than love for the sinner is itself a sin against justice and charity.

In and of itself, however, that is not likely to satisfy the new reformers. Doesn't that simply amount to the old bromide that we are to love the sinner, but hate the sin? And doesn't that mean in turn that we are justified in hating and rejecting every sinful action through and through, in all its parts, and without reservation? How do we perform the feat of mental gymnastics that enables us to separate the person from the act? Does not the person enter into the act, and does not the act characterize the person?

Aquinas would reply, I believe, that the new reformers are right! We cannot separate the person from the act. A truly human act (as opposed to a "tic" or a "knee-jerk") is an actualization of the powers of the soul, and therefore of the person. Hence we are not to hate the sinful act; we are to hate what is sinful *in* the act. The distinction is not a minor one, simply another instance of scholastic nit-picking. It goes to the heart of the doctrine of creation and to the very heart of human action itself. All created reality is ordered to God, and everything that has being points to him. Even the most sinful human act is ordered to God—whether the agent knows it or not. For ultimately, according to Aquinas, every human act is ordered to the attainment of something that in and of itself is really good. And God contains in himself the perfection of every good. In seeking something that is truly good, we seek God—whether we know it or not! "You have made me for yourself, and my heart is not at rest until it rests in you." That holds of the sinner as well as of the saint.

"Every human act is ultimately ordered to the attainment of something that in and of itself is really good." That is the heart of Aquinas's analysis of human motivation. Therefore the starting point of any moral analysis is identifying the good that the agent wants ultimately to achieve or obtain. If we cannot find such a good—if our attempts to do so terminate unavoidably in the judgment that the agent wants nothing else, for example, than to cause pain—then we must conclude that the agent is either pathological or possessed by demons. In either case, the ordinary process of moral analysis and evaluation has become irrelevant and other sorts of actions are called for.

If the ultimate intention of any human act is to achieve or obtain something that in and of itself is really good, and something that can be recognized as such by all rational men and women, then a fundamental task of moral analysis is to give an account of the ways that evil may enter into human actions. Aquinas never talks about "evil actions." He talks instead about the evil *in* actions. Far from ignoring the new reformers' demand that we pay attention to what is good in morally deficient acts, Aquinas considers the evil in human acts as a vitiation of the good. Evil cannot exist in its own right. Therefore it cannot totally destroy the goodness in any human act. Evil enters into an act—it vitiates an act—when an agent pursues something good in an inordinate way. It is my contention that every instance of a morally deficient sexual act is an instance of the inordinate pursuit of something that in and of itself is really good. To that extent, I believe, there is material agreement between the new reformers and traditional moralists. It is time now to locate the important differences between them. And to do that, we must turn to particular cases. I shall begin our case studies in what might seem a most surprising manner. I shall discuss masturbation.

I have chosen that class of traditionally forbidden sexual acts precisely because it has become so marginal to contemporary discussions of the ethics of sexuality. No one, I hope, will draw the conclusion that I want to return to the days when adolescents were terrified by thunderous moral condemnations of "spilling one's seed." We all know that at a certain time in life the vast majority of human beings are going to masturbate, and I for one do not intend to lose any sleep over the matter. And yet, just because there is so little concern these days about masturbation, it provides a good case for clarifying what is and what is not necessarily implied by the claim that a certain sort of sexual act is "vitiated" or "morally deficient." It also provides a splendid opportunity to illustrate the differences between a moral analysis based on a model of human nature as social through and through, and one based on the individualistic and naturalistic model. Let's see what happens, then, when we address Aquinas's pragmatic questions to an act of masturbation.

I shall leave to the reader's imagination the answer to Aristotle's question, "What exactly did he do?" We can specify that aspect of the act by describing what Aquinas calls its terminus, or object. The answer is that he acted in such a way as to produce a solitary orgasm and ejaculation. Up to this point, the "he" in question could very well be a dog! Therefore, the next relevant question is, "Who is he?" (The relevant order in which to raise the usual list of Aristotelian questions varies from case to case.) Assuming that we are speaking of a human being, the answer to that question will include specifications of his age, the stage of his emotional, intellectual, and physical development, and his state of awareness at the time. The reason that the answers to this question are important is that without them we do not know how to understand the most important question in the list, "Why did he do it?"

There is one sense in which we could answer that question even in the case of a dog: "To experience the gratification and pleasure that orgasm and ejaculation bring on the heels of an experience of sexual craving." Unlike certain late-medieval moralists, we should not hold the dog morally responsible, or raise the question of morality at all. In order to raise the question of moral responsibility, it is not sufficient to ascribe to the agent some sort of understandable natural inclination. A morally responsible agent must have a reason for his action; he must be consciously motivated. He must have knowledge of the good that he is seeking, and believe that a certain kind of intentional action is likely to produce or facilitate the attaining of that good. He must then deliberately decide to embark on that course of action.

That is why it is important to know the age, the stage of emotional, intellectual, and physical development, and the state of awareness of the agent. The answers to those questions are relevant to determining the extent to which the act was fully reasoned and deliberate—the extent to which moral analysis is possible at all. For Aquinas, the closer we can come to fully explaining and understanding an action by reference to a "natural" inclination to gratify "natural" cravings, the further we are from a truly human act where moral analysis is even possible! The contrast with the modern model of human motivation, which bases reasonableness and ethical justification on precisely that inclination, could not be clearer.

But now let's suppose that we are dealing with a fully mature adult male, who with full awareness considers the possibility of achieving the sexual gratification and pleasure that a solitary orgasm and ejaculation will produce, deliberately sets out on a course of action that first induces sexual arousal, and finally terminates in the desired objective. How is his action to be morally analyzed and evaluated? Was it morally good or morally deficient? For Aquinas, it cannot be morally neutral, since in the absence of any vitiating factor it is positively virtuous to pursue an available good. Was there a vitiating factor in his action? While I still will not lose any sleep over the matter, I believe that the correct answer is that there was indeed a vitiating factor—more than one, in fact—and that the act was morally deficient. How might such a claim be reasonably defended, and what implications could it possibly have for the way in which we are to conceive of the single life?

Let's begin by asking what good it was to which the act of masturbation was consciously and volitionally ordered. There are two kinds of possible answers. First, the agent simply thought of the sexual gratification and pleasure that he might obtain by means of his act, and decided to pursue the course of action that would terminate in that objective. Second, the agent was tense and sexually frustrated. He knew that in his current state he would not be able to complete a piece of work that was needed by his fellow workers for the completion of a serum to save hundreds of infected children from imminent death. In order to facilitate his work toward that socially desirable end, he engaged in an act of masturbation. What should we say of the two cases?

In the first case, Aquinas's answer is immediately clear. The experience of sexual gratification is good. But it is not an "intelligible" good—not the sort of good that in and of itself provides a rational reason for action. It is a good that we are rationally and morally justified in seeking only in the context of pursuing some good external to or consequent upon the sexual act itself, such as the unity of husband and wife, the procreation of children, or the stability of the social order. Why would Aquinas argue in that fashion? It is not that he has anything against psycho-physiological urges. It is a matter of character and the common good. The kinds of actions in which we indulge affect our moral character, tending to produce in us habitual patterns of action—habitual dispositions to pursue and prefer some goods above others.

The person who practices the pursuit of individual gratification as an end in itself is less likely to be disposed, by second nature, as it were, to pursue and prefer the common good of all of the members of his or her community, than is the person who habitually subordinates the pursuit of individual gratification to the pursuit of social goods. That is why, for Aquinas, any pattern of sexual behaviour that systematically excludes any one of the external social goods associated with sexual acts— the unity of husband and wife, the procreation of children, or the stability of the social order—is to that extent morally deficient. By nature (our true, acquired social nature) our sexual actions are ordered to all of those goods, and the systematic exclusion of any one of them renders our actions less socially fecund than they might be. The virtue of temperance— a habitual disposition to subordinate the pursuit of one's individual gratification to the pursuit of social (and therefore intelligible) goods—is ultimately instrumental to, and in the service of, the virtue of justice. Ultimately, of course, in pursuing a just and peaceful community, that common good to which all virtuous actions are ordered, I am simultaneously pursuing my own real and natural earthly good.

Now, and more briefly, what are we to say of the man who indulges in an act of masturbation for the sake of contributing greatly to the common good of his society? Aquinas would distinguish between the end that he sought through his action, and the action itself considered as a means to that end. With regard to the action itself, Aquinas would have to say that it possesses the same moral deficiency as found in the first case. To masturbate, the man had to put his ultimate end out of his mind, and fantasize about the sexual use of some human being, with the desired objective of experiencing the same internal goods of sexual gratification and pleasure as were sought by the man in the first case. As a means toward his noble end, he would have to indulge seriously and wholemindedly in a practice that objectively tends to undermine his moral character.

But Aquinas would not stop there. While the end does not justify the means, or magically eliminate the objective deficiency of the chosen act, the goodness of the end pursued "flows into" the act itself, and moderates its vitiated character. The second agent is more praiseworthy, or less blameworthy, than the first. The intended end and the chosen means are not finally separable or independent of one another. But their distinction for purposes of analysis allows for a more nuanced judgment, I should claim, than is likely to be available to either the traditional moralizer or the new reformer.

And now, if we were to run down the list of controversial proposals put forward by the new reformers, it should be clear what sorts of judgments a traditional moralist such as Aquinas would be constrained to make. It would first be granted that every one of the sexual acts for which the new reformers propose a new and positive moral evaluation is ultimately ordered to the pursuit of some real good. Otherwise, it is not a human act at all, but a manifestation of pathology or demonic possession, and so we can stop our moral evaluation of that particular act right there. We then ask, "Is the nature of the deliberately chosen act itself such that it tends to produce in the agent dispositions of character conducive to to the pursuit and preference of social goods over individual goods?" If there is *any* aspect of the act that tends to undermine the pursuit of social goods, then the act is vitiated and morally deficient.

Such a deficiency may enter in in many ways—through the immediate end that the agent desires to achieve by means of the action, through some higher end to which the immediate end is subordinated, or through the very nature of the act itself, considered as a deliberately chosen means to the intended end. In each case, however, the criteria of judgment are social. It is a matter of the character of the agent considered as a member of the community bound to seek its commmon good. And it is a matter of the nature of the intended end of the action, and its contribution to, or undermining of, the common good. The moral analysis and the moral evaluation is social through and through. But the final judgment will never be an un-nuanced condemnation. It will be a function of identifying any element that vitiates the act from the point of view of social goods, while recognizing the goods present in it as elements that may affect the degree of praiseworthiness or blamewor-thiness that is due to the agent. One thing remains constant and unchangeable. If there is a vitiating factor of any kind within the action or within its intended ends, the act can never be morally "right"—it will always "wrong" knowingly and in-tentionally to perform such an act.

In terms of acts that might be performed within the context of the single life, any act that is ordered solely to the achieve-ment of the internal and individual goods of sexual gratification and pleasure is vitiated and morally deficient. Any sexual act that systematically excludes any of the external social goods of the unity of man and wife, the procreation and education of children, and the stability of the social order is objectively vitiated and morally deficient. Since no one possesses any natural rights in the modern sense, that is, totally apart from social institutions and the goods that they define, no one has a natural right to sexual gratification and pleasure, or a natural right to have a child. Since sexual practices that systematically exclude any of the external goods that justify seeking sexual gratification and pleasure are themselves to that extent vitiated, it would seem that homosexual practices also are "morally deficient," whatever goods they may otherwise con-tain, or whatever good and noble intentions may flow into them to counterbalance their moral deficiency. But what the tradi-tional moralist is really saying is that in the context of the single life *any* acts that are ordered to the sexual gratification and pleasure induced by orgasm are objectively vitiated and morally deficient. It is not in accord with right reason to indulge in them. Moral judgments, however, must be nuanced, as the vitiating factors are weighed against the good that may flow into them from truly loving and noble intentions. And above all those who indulge in them must be loved with the unremitting love of charity, in full awareness of the fact that a person can never be wholly separated from his or her acts. All such acts, however, remain objectively vitiated and morally deficient, and the church can neither bless nor condone them. To do so would be to undermine both the moral character of individuals and the common good of the community.

Have we placed such constraints on the single life that we are denying to those who have not yet married, those who will never marry, or those who, for whatever reason, find themselves once again unmarried, the possibility of some good to which they have just claim and should be encouraged to pursue? If the model of human nature presupposed by such traditional moralists such as Aquinas, Hooker, and Taylor is realistic, then that is not the case. On the contrary, we are encouraging them to pursue precisely those virtues, those dispositions of character, that are conducive to the common good. For all of our truly natural rights derive from a common life in a just and peaceful society.

Needless to say, I do not expect my arguments here to be convincing to the new reformers or to a growing majority of our youth. It is little more than the sketch of an alternative model of human nature and human motivation—one that differs radically from the individualistic and naturalistic model dominant in our culture. There are no hard rules of rationality to which I can appeal. All that I, or any other supporter of traditional morality can do is ask the new reformers and the modern libertarians to look again at their model and ask themselves seriously if it can be used to justify the pursuit of a just and peaceful society which is anything other than a context for the unbridled pursuit of human gratification and pleasure. And I can also ask them if they honestly believe that such a pursuit of gratification is conducive to the sort of character they themselves would like their friends and neighbors to possess. The model of human nature they use to justify their demands for radical change in traditional sexual ethics may be in some sense compatible with virtuous character, loving relations, and a just social order, but it is in no way conducive to such goods.

IV

Until now my argument has been almost entirely devoid of a theological or biblical dimension. I have been discussing how we might pursue our created earthly good. Just as I believe, however, that "nature" as it is defined by our culture must be subordinated to a model of human nature ordered to the true social goods of justice and peace, so I also believe that the natural social nature of human beings must be subordinated to what what the new reformers misleadingly call the Christian "ideal." Christians believe with Aquinas that men and women are called not only be be virtuous citizens of earthly communities, but fundamentally to be "fellow citizens with the saints in heaven."

In other words, they are called to what the Orthodox term "divinization," a participation in the very life of the Triune God. That call, for me, provides what rational argument may not: a decisive reason for rejecting the individualistic and naturalistic model of human nature that informs so much of our ethical discourse. The life to which we are called, the life of the Triune God, is a life of eternal community, informed and unified by the power of love. It is a life within which the affirmation of the being and good of one is the affirmation of the being and good of all. That model—not a model of human nature, but of the Nature to which we are ordered—has served for several thousand years to call human beings to goods that surpass those of individual gratification and pleasure. I put more trust in it than I do in Aquinas's social model of human nature, or any other model based on the natural loves and motivations of human beings.

Nothing I find in any human model, whether that of Aquinas or of our modern liberal culture, seems to me to offer anything that even approaches a good reason to abandon the traditional interpretation of Scripture or the Christian tradition of sexual ethics derived from it. Anything that might appear to offer a good reason to abandon those traditional teachings would, on the same grounds, constitute an equally good reason for abandoning the church's traditional teachings concerning justice or any other social virtue that leads to the pursuit of a common good beyond our individual gratification and pleasure.

When men and women come to face the choice of whether to remain within that institution we now call the singe life, or to enter that alternative institution we call marriage, the theological and scriptural model of Nature provides a sanction for each. It gives sacramental character to both states of life by ordering the goods of each to that Good which is their source and archetype. If the proper goods of the single life and the proper goods of matrimony are each ordered to the Good that constitutes the being in unity of the eternal Trinity, then there is no justification in either of those states of life for putting the pursuit of individual goods above the pursuit of social goods. Only the pursuit of the common good of men and women together, and of all other earthly goods for their sake, provides the proper matter for the graceful operation of divinely inspired charity.

That good may be sought either in marriage or in the single life that intrinsically remains open to the possibility of marriage. There is only one other alternative: a celibate life that intentionally closes off the possibilities of marriage for the sake of stability in the pursuit of those goods common to all men and women, married and unmarried. All three states of life may be equally and fully lived in the pursuit of the common good on earth of the people of God, in preparation for the enjoyment of that One and Three that constitutes the eternal good of the community of the saints.

LOVE, MARRIAGE, AND FRIENDSHIP

Elizabeth Zarelli Turner

I

In the final scene of D. H. Lawrence's novel *Women in Love*, Birkin stares at the frozen corpse of his friend Gerald and says, "He should have loved me; I offered him!"

Birkin's lover Ursula asks him if he needs Gerald and he responds, "Yes."

"Aren't I enough for you?" she asks.

"No. You are enough for me, as far as a woman is concerned. You are all women to me. But I wanted a man friend, as eternal as you and I are eternal . . . ."

"You can't have two kinds of love. Why should you?"

"It seems as if I can't. Yet I wanted it."

"You can't have it, because it's false, impossible," she said.

"I don't believe that," he answered.[1]

This conversation between Birkin and Ursula about the possibility of two kinds of love, friendship and erotic love, poses the question of this chapter: what is the relationship between friendship and erotic love in relationships between men and women? Are friendship and the love between husband and wife synonymous loves? To what extent is friendship between men and women the basis for marriage? To what extent is such friendship possible?

The answers to these questions may seem obvious, particularly given the frequency with which friendship is mentioned as the reason for a couple's decision to marry ("I'm marrying my best friend!"). In her chapter "Two Shall Become One," Helen Oppenheimer contends that "a good marriage develops either from friendship or into friendship." She also, however, points to the problem of a sexual ethic based on friendship which then attempts to add sex and the injunction "to forsake all others" to the mix. The result is either a distorted definition of friendship, which makes it both exclusive and sexual, or a distorted view of marriage, which makes it essentially non-sexual and non-exclusive. Friendship between members of the opposite sex is either extolled as the basis for marriage or minimized in an effort to deny any sexual involvement ("We're just friends!").

It is clearly the dominant expectation of American culture that a couple be friends as well as lovers. Although the dominance of this expectation is a fairly recent development in understanding the marriage bond, it is by no means solely contemporary. In the thirteenth century Thomas Aquinas asserted that "the form of matrimony consists in an inseparable union of minds, a couple are pledged to one another in faithful friendship."[2] The question remains, however, to what extent friendship and marriage are related. The limitations of our culture's expectations for love and friendship must be explored and tested lest we diminish the value of either friendship or the marriage bond.

It is my contention that friendship and the marriage bond have become so closely linked because of interpretive shifts in the way these two kinds of love are conceived. These shifts have had both positive and negative effects on the social institutions of both marriage and friendship. Like D. H. Lawrence's Ursula, we have believed that two kinds of love are essentially impossible and so in reaction we have made the two nearly coterminous. Friendship was once considered the highest form of love, the subject of serious ethical and theological inquiry. In the past several hundred years moral philosophers, ethicists and theologians have overlooked friendship's value. Suggested reasons for this oversight include the emphasis placed on marriage and erotic relationships between men and women in ethical reflection; our own contemporary preoccupation with work, which allows less time for developing and enjoying friendship; ethical reflection that has focused on social duties and obligations rather than on relationships freely chosen;[3] and our obsession with the isolation and fragmentation engendered by a post-industrial, technological culture.[4] Whatever the reasons, "friend" describes relationships as casual as an acquaintance or as intimate as a spouse. It can as easily be used to describe the one for whom I would give my life or the one who may be "out of sight, out of mind." There is no single or pure definition of friendship to which we can turn, but an examination of historical and theological sources provides a framework for discussing the similarities and the dissimilarities between friendship, erotic love and the marriage bond as we now understand them.

Before proceeding to an examination of the sources it is imperative to note a significant limitation: prior to comparatively recent literature, most major essays on friendship have been written by men and about their friendship with other men. Very little attention has been paid to friendship among women, or to friendship between women and men. This may partially be explained by the attitude displayed by Montaigne in the sixteenth century, who contended that women were by nature incapable of friendship. He thought that women could not withstand the tremendous demands of friendship—the pressure of such a permanent relationship. He also said, however, that if women *were* capable of friendship it would be more full and complete than it was among men. And because friendship assumed equality, friendships between women and men were generally assumed impossible in those times and cultures which maintained the inequality of the sexes.

One notable exception seems to be friendships that flourished within monastic communities, particularly during the 12th and 13th centuries. In *Friendship and Community: The Monastic Experience 350-1250*, Brian Patrick McGuire observes that as monastic male friendships eroded in the 13th century, friendships between religious men and women appeared. The written correspondence between the Dominicans Jordan of Saxony and Diana of Andalo illustrates such a friendship. The existence of such correspondence and of such friendships does relatively little, nevertheless, to broaden the limitation of the philosophically analytical sources. There is no longer any question about the ability of women, or of women and men, to form friendships, nor is it my purpose to offer an exhaustive treatise on friendship. Rather, this essay is an attempt to reclaim a definition of friendship which will restore its value and which will clarify the distinctions and similarities between friendship, erotic love and marriage.

Such a definition can best be reclaimed by first surveying several classical and theological sources which deal with friendship. By doing so we can discover those essential elements which must be considered in adapting material written primarily about male bonds of affection to the male-female relationships presently under consideration. The following overview will serve as the basis for analysis of the relationship between friendship, love and marriage.

II

The classic and most significant theses on friendship come from the ancient civilizations of Greece and Rome. These theses reflect assumptions common to several ancients texts, as well as adaptations and differences which reflect the various political, sociological, philosophical and religious contexts of the various authors. Plato, Aristotle, Cicero and Plutarch each wrote major works on friendship. It is the latter three who particularly require our attention, both because of the value they place on that particular relationship and because of the influence their reflections have had on subsequent Christian and non-Christian considerations of friendship. Yet Plato must be mentioned as well because his formulation of friendship reemerges in the thought of St. Augustine, thereby exerting a continuing influence on Christian assessments of love, marriage and friendship.

Much of Plato's theory of friendship is contained in three works, *Lysis*, *Symposium*, and *Phaedrus*. In each of these he raises questions common to other reflections on friendship. He asks, for example, if friendship is always mutual, if it is permanent, if it must be reciprocated, and if it is a relationship between lovers or non-lovers. He concludes that friends are best chosen from among non-lovers, that they must be similar insofar as they have congenial natures, and that friendship is both mutual and reciprocated. Permanence is not of particular importance, however, in Plato's scheme. There are two primary reasons why this is the case. The first is that Plato envisioned friendship primarily as a relationship between mentor and student; because students come and go, permanence was essentially an impossibility. The second reason is the most substantial and is at the core of all Plato's philosophy: friendship is essentially an opportunity for beholding and loving beauty in another, as one step towards the ultimate goal of loving beauty wherever it may be found. Particular attachments are not permanent and must be transcended so that they do not become a hindrance in the greater search for truth and beauty. Friends are interchangeable insofar as they all facilitate the greater love.

However casually we might refer to *friends* and *friendship*, however, we still assume that the particular relationship is of importance in itself and not simply as a means toward the end of some greater goal or more significant love. friendship as a particular relationship that is of value in itself is treated seriously by Plato in his later works, and also by Aristotle, Cicero and Plutarch.

Aristotle's precise formulation of a theory of friendship is contained most succinctly in Books VIII and IX of *Nichomachean Ethics*. For Aristotle friendship is a preferential relationship; friends are not at all interchangeable in the way Plato suggested. Whereas for Plato a friend represented something not present in oneself, for Aristotle a friend is in some sense another self: friendship exists between those who are both good and alike with respect to virtue. Friendships are carefully chosen, preferential, and limited in number.

Friendship is also something required by all. According to Aristotle, the wealthy and powerful need friends to guard them from error; the old need their attention and support; those in the prime of life need friends to enable them to do noble actions; the poor need friends as a refuge from their poverty.[5]

Aristotle picks up Plato's question about whether or not friends must be similar to one another. He approaches the question by suggesting that there are three major classifications of friends. Friendship exists by virtue of three primary attributes: what is useful, what is pleasant, and what is good. A friend may be loved for any of these attributes, but perfect friendship exists only when a person is loved by virtue of the good. Goodness, or virtue, is stable; pleasure and usefulness are variable. Permanence and stability in friendship are only possible and assured when two people are friends by virtue of the good in one another; by virtue of who or what they are rather than because of what they can offer.

Equality is another mandatory requirement for friendship of the highest, most perfect sort. Whereas Plato suggested that friendship more frequently occurred in the unequal relationship between mentor and student, Aristotle asserts that equality and goodness are most conducive to lasting friendship. The highest form of friendship exists when those who are equal choose one another as friends because of the equality of the other's character.[6]

This shift in emphasis toward the value of equality illustrates the way in which the definition and functions of friendship are sociologically and culturally determined. Whereas Plato seems to have envisioned friendships within an educational context, thereby adopting the mentor-student relationship as a primary model, Aristotle's version of friendship has its roots in the equal relations that existed between citizens of the *polis*. He considered friendship a political necessity, the means whereby men were able to live and function in society. Friendship was considered the glue which held a state together, for "when men are friends, they have no need of justice at all, but when they are just they still need friendship."[7] The unity of the state was thought to be maintained by friendship among men of virtue. Such men, according to Aristotle, will not be guilty of slander or factionalism; they will refuse to slander their friends and will wish each other's good, politically and individually.

In Book IX of the *Nichomachean Ethics* Aristotle identifies four characteristics of a friend and says that at least two of the four must be present if the friendship is true. These four characteristics are: to desire what is good for the sake of the other; to desire that the other live for his own sake; to enjoy passing time with and choosing the same things as the other; and to share the other's sorrows and joys.

Aristotle also contended that perfect friendship incurs moral obligation. A person has a greater obligation to be just to a friend than to a stranger—what is justice towards a friend differs from justice towards a stranger or an acquaintance. The justice or injustice of an act is partially determined by the nature of the relationship which exists between the parties involved. Thus, although it is never just to defraud another of their money, it is a more egregious offense when done to a friend than to a stranger. As a special relationship, friendship warrants special regard, even though that regard must not violate or negate other moral obligations towards one's family or toward the community.

Although a person may have numerous friendships based on pleasure or utility, perfect friendships based on virtue are rare because of the time and familiarity they presuppose. Perfect friendships assume a permanence which can survive distance or conflict. They are to be broken only if the character of the friend is altered in such a way as to be no longer good or virtuous.

Cicero's notion of friendship, as he articulated it in *De Amicitia*, was, like Aristotle's, rooted in politics. Friendship was the cohesive and organizational factor in the Roman political structure. For Cicero, the essence of friendship resides in agreement and similarity: complete agreement in policy, goals and opinions is essential. The political dimension of friendship, however, is not isolated from the more personal and intimate dimensions. Cicero simply assumed that friends are chosen within the political arena. This is because friendship was restricted to the *boni*, to those who are good; such virtue was also assumed of those who were members of the Roman ruling class. According to Cicero, "Friendship is nothing else than an accord in all things human and divine, conjoined with mutual good will and affection."[8]

Friendships maintain political unity, accord, harmony and stability. They are also eternal and must be preserved with utmost loyalty, fidelity, constancy and justice. Unlike Aristotle, Cicero did not allow for variable friendships based on utility or pleasure: they must be perfect friendships, carefully chosen, tested, and appraised before the person is loved as a friend. This permanence and test of character were essential for political stability and security; one must always be on the lookout for troubles that may befall the state, either externally or internally. Friends must request and do only that which is honorable, lest political stability be imperiled.

For Cicero the three most important characteristics of friendship are virtue, loyalty and equality. Virtue—harmony, permanence and fidelity— creates and preserves the bond of friendship. Without virtue friendship cannot exist, and for this reason it is only possible among the virtuous and must be ever maintained. Loyalty is the support and stay of constancy in friendship. equality is of utmost importance; if not already present in the relationship, it must be created, and one of the friends may need to assume a lower status for this to be effected. Friends must be carefully chosen, but friendship is not something a person may choose to do without. It is necessary for political life and for life itself. Cicero thought that to take friendship from life would be like taking the sun from the universe.[9]

Plutarch's major contribution to the discussion of friendship is his conviction that it is impossible to have numerous friends. This conviction is the theme of his essay, "On Having Many Friends." The duties and obligations of friendship are the primary restrictive factors which prevent the accumulation of a multitude of friends. There is an obligation to maintain the friendships we have, to be loyal and faithful. We dare not risk losing friends in the process of seeking new ones, nor dare we risk spreading affection in too many places. Like Cicero, Plutarch contended that friendship must be tried and tested before making a commitment to the relationship. Such a period of judgment demands time and energy, and is necessary if the obligation to preserve the permanence of friendship is to be honored.

A multitude of friends also raises the question of conflicting obligations. Plutarch observes that we run the risk of having friends request the same things at the same time, while being unable to meet any of the requests. We also run the risk of having the several friends call us to different tasks or journeys at the same time: it is "impossible to be with them all, and unnatural to be with none, and yet to do service to one alone, and thus to offend many."[10] There is an obligation to treat one's friends with equal regard; to do so, one must weigh the demands of friendship over what friendship might bestow. If we emphasize the good we receive from friendship, it would be most valuable to have a host of friends. But if we emphasize the demands put on us by friendship's obligations, we soon realize that our energy is better focused on a restricted number of intimate friends.

Plutarch presents an adaptation of Aristotle's three-fold classification of friendship. He claims that friendship seeks after three things above all else: virtue as a good thing, intimacy as a pleasant thing, and usefulness as a necessary thing.[11] Although the first is clearly the most important, the three are not presented as different levels or sorts of friendship, with only one representing the pure or true form. Rather, all three are intrinsic to friendship. In Plutarch's scheme, the lesser friendship is one that is shared with too many others or is casually embraced without the prerequisite period of judgment and testing. A person who attempts to acquire many friends is a "soul that is very impressionable, versatile, pliant and readily changeable." True friendship is rare because of the requisite virtue: a steady character which does not shift about but continues in one intimacy.

III

Despite the cultural and political diversity represented by these sources, a fairly consistent portrait of friendship emerges that is to remain constant throughout subsequent literature. Even though there is written correspondence between men and women (as between the above-mentioned Jordan and Diana, and between Saints Francis and Clare) which reflects close bonds of friendship, the literature primarily assumes that friendship is a bond between people of the same sex. It is a preferential and a fairly exclusive relationship: friends are carefully chosen, take priority over certain other relationships, and are limited in number. They are limited in number because of the time and energy required in building and maintaining them (friends choose to do things together and spend time sharing each others' sorrows and joys) and also because of the moral obligation attendant upon them. Cicero observed that true friendships are difficult to find because of the difficulty of finding someone who prefers a friend's advancement to his own, and who will descend to calamity's depths for another. Friendship is itself a virtue and requires such virtue as loyalty, fidelity and justice to preserve the permanence of the bond. Even though it is meant to be a permanent relationship, it may be severed if pleasure or utility has been its basis, or if the character of one of the friends is altered in such a way that differences rather than similarities dominate, or if one of them is no longer virtuous. equality, mutuality and reciprocity are requisite for friendship. Friendship assumes a similarity in character, virtue and world-view.

Friendship is a personal bond but it is not a private relationship: the moral obligations of friendship extend to the political, sociological, religious, etc., environment in which the friends find themselves. Aristotle and Cicero were explicit about the centrality of friendship for the stability of the state. In Christian communities, about which more will be said later, friendship clearly was not simply a private matter. It was seen either as a threat to the unity of the body and a violation of the command to love *all* as God has loved us, or it was valued and encouraged as a school of charity, crucial to the life of the community, and paradigmatic of our friendship with God. Friendship affected, and was affected by, the prevailing culture in respect both to its definition and its duties.

Finally, friendship is a non-sexual relationship. In the *Phaedrus* Plato said that friends are best chosen from among non-lovers, because lovers have their judgment obscured by passion and try to keep the beloved in an inferior position. This has, perhaps, been the most controversial characteristic of friendship because the intimacy and passion of the relationship has often been misconstrued as sexual intimacy and passion. It is the souls of friends that become united, and not their bodies. But the language describing friendship is often similar to that describing the relationship between lovers. And so, when David grieves over the death of his friend Jonathan he says, "Your love for me was wonderful, more wonderful than that of women" (II Sam. 1:26). And when Ruth is told by Naomi to return to her own people, she says, "Don't urge me to leave you or to turn back from you. Where you go I will go, and where you stay I will stay. Your people will be my people and your God my God. . . . May the Lord deal with me, be it ever so severely, if anything but death separate you and me" (Ruth 1:16-17). I have heard speculation that David and Jonathan were lovers because of the intensity of their relationship, and Ruth's plea to her friend has become a promise made by women and men to one another. Nearly every account of friendship has been written by someone who loved a friend with heart, mind and soul, and many accounts have been written in that period of grief when the loss of a friend is being mourned. Friends may be carefully chosen and tested in what may seem an objective way, but once the other is loved as a friend it is a relationship of considerable intensity and passion. What other language have we to describe such intensity than the language of love?

This portrait of friendship is essentially that assumed by Christian authors. The reinterpretation occurs in the description of the context in which friendship exists and in the interpretation of the significance of the relationship. Christians, like the ancient Greeks and Romans, did not consider friendship to be a private bond in isolation from a larger community. They were, however, uniquely concerned about its relationship to their fidelity to the call to discipleship and to the vision of a community in which "the company of those who believed were of one heart and soul, and no one said that any of the things which he possessed was his own, but they had everything in common" (Acts 4:32). All human relationships were to be judged according to the standard of their effect on the believers' relationship with God and with one another.

Little was written about friendship prior to the Constantinian settlement of the fourth century. It is not surprising that those early Christians had little to say about establishing permanent relationships, when their expectation and prayer was that the Lord would soon return. St. Paul is clear in his First Letter to the Corinthians that because "the appointed time has grown very short" (I Cor. 7:29) the faithful should remain in whatever state they are in, married or single. He also makes it clear that those who are unmarried have the advantage of undivided interests and need worry solely about pleasing the Lord. The married, however, are "anxious about worldly affairs," about how to please husbands and wives. Undivided devotion to the Lord is clearly the greatest good and St. Paul indicates that such devotion is most possible for those without domestic obligation.

When friendship becomes a topic for theological considera- tion in the fourth century, it is interpreted by the Eastern church fathers as a relationship to be avoided and by the Western church fathers as one to be valued when rightly ordered. The Eastern desert fathers interpreted the injunction to leave all and follow quite literally: they moved from their villages to the desert and lived as simply as possible either as hermits or as monks occupying individual cells within cenobitic monasteries. Friendships that formed within the monasteries were not disallowed, but neither were the monks encouraged to forge human bonds with any but their spiritual fathers. As Jesus was alone in the wilderness during his temptation, so did these desert monks seek solitude to have their faith tested, to give themselves completely to a life of prayer, and to break those worldly attachments which were thought to hinder or prevent the formation of spiritual bonds. Friendships which presumed a preference for one person over another were seen as worldly attachments which violated the requirement that all be loved equally as brothers and sisters. Saint Basil the Great's argument against preferential or par- ticular friendships was that such bonds created a community within a community and were thereby divisive and harmful to the life of the entire community. Basil's suspicion of friendship was a suspicion widely accepted by Eastern monasticism. Far from being the glue of society Aristotle thought it to be, friendship was interpreted as detrimental to the integrity of the spiritual society the desert monks sought to build.

The Eastern church's concerns about the integrity of the community and the negative impact particular friendships may have on community life are reflected in the writings of the West, yet there friendship is also interpreted in a positive light. As was the case in the East, the monastery became the primary locus within the Christian community where friendship acquired particular significance. In the West, friendship was viewed in a more positive light, as a metaphor for life together in community, and as a metaphor for life with God. Eastern asceticism was studied and respected by Western monastics, but the ascetic rigor was not emulated. Rather than seeking solitude and isolation, religious women and men in the West sought to build a new *polis*: the City of God, the community of the faithful. They did not completely abandon their former lives, but struggled to relate ancient, contemporary and Christian ways of life to their new life in God. And so in much of the Christian literature we see the Ciceronian notion of friendship as an intimate bond and as a political means for ensuring harmony, stability and unity. The goal was always the unity of the Body of Christ, and friendship was a suitable model and metaphor for relationships to the extent that it maintained that unity.

One of the major concerns that emerged about friendship, and about all relationships, was that they be rightly ordered. Whereas for Aristotle friendship took precedence over love for one's fellow citizens, such could not be the case in a Christian community where fidelity to God was primary. This obligation to love and obedience included allowing God to determine the pattern for relationships. It was St. Augustine who most em-

phatically and clearly articulated a theology of the right ordering of love. According to Augustine, God has made us for
himself; God is the goal of life. The Christian life is a life of
learning to love rightly, putting first the love of God which is
the greatest of virtues. All other loves, no matter how splendid
or noble they may be, if not so ordered, are merely "splendid
vices." He considered friendship "a delightful bond" but one
which may be occasion for sin if it causes abandonment of
"those higher and better things, your truth, your law, and you
yourself."[12] Augustine's understanding of the significance of
friendship was similar to Plato's: friendship was a sign and call
to the love of God. Because God is the goal of life, love of a
friend must turn from the friend to God. Friends must be loved
in God and not in themselves, for all things are from him and
reside in him.[13] Nevertheless, he affirmed the value and necessity of preferential relationships as well as the greater necessity for universal love; that charity which embraces both friend
and enemy in the love of God.

The most comprehensive and therefore significant early
Christian reflection on friendship was written by Aelred of
Rievaulx in the twelfth century. Aelred's *Spiritual Friendship*
was the product of an age in which monastic friendships were
highly valued. It also marks the final stage of such positive
interpretations of friendship; the early Eastern suspicion of
particular friendships regained dominance and monastic communities discouraged friendships for reasons of divisiveness
and dissension. Aelred's reliance on ancient texts is evident:
he modeled his work on Cicero's *De Amicitia*. Again, it is not
the particular elements of friendship which are altered, but the
significance of friendship is adapted to reflect the right ordering of love. Friendship, for Aelred, is the means whereby one

abides in God, and God in them. To be a friend to others makes one a friend of God. As in Augustinian theology, friendship comes from and returns to God; it is the means whereby we effect our return to God.

IV

There has certainly been more Christian reflection on friendship than is evident in my brief synopsis of only a few sources. I have merely attempted to lay a foundation of essential elements and common themes basic to any discussion of friendship. We leaped from St. Augustine in the fifth century to Aelred in the twelfth, and now we leap from the twelfth to the twentieth century, to contemporary reflections on friendship and marriage.

Friendship is no longer rooted in the soil of the *polis* or of the monastery. Discussions about the unity of the Body of Christ no longer seriously consider friendship as a factor of its unity or disunity. Friendships and sexual relationships are now discussed in terms of ministry to those who are single, married, with or without children, or else in terms of how best to include those with "alternative lifestyles" (however vaguely or specifically those lifestyles may be defined) into a parish "family." Friendship has essentially lost its sociological context and become almost solely a private, intimate bond.

Vestiges of the sociological weight of friendship are nevertheless visible, particularly in the response friendships often elicit within the communities in which they are formed. Because friendship is a preferential relationship, those who are not chosen to be someone's friend may become envious of the friendship. The Eastern ascetics' suspicions about the formation of a community within a community persist in the work place and in the church. Because intimacy and sexual relations are generally assumed to be so closely linked, there is often an immediate suspicion or assumption that intimate friends are also lovers. This is further confused by the fact that "friend" has become a popular euphemism for referring to a sexual partner to whom one is not married. Friendships may also be seen as a threat to family obligations or priorities: parents may resent time children choose to give to friends at the presumed neglect of family members, or spouses may resent the priority a friend may receive. As isolated and as demanding as much of contemporary life seems to be, we still seek to form intimate bonds of friendship, love and marriage, and those bonds are formed within some broader context than the privacy of individual lives.

Suffice it to say, however, that no single context can be assumed for these relationships, nor any single model adopted. We no longer assume that married people share the same home, or even the same city. The *New York Times* recently reported that in 1987, 758,000 married women lived apart from their husbands for reasons other than marital discord or military service. An article in the *Cincinnati Enquirer* a few years ago reported that married couples who do live together spend an average of fifteen minutes a week in conversation about matters of import. Psychiatrists are as likely, if not more so, to be granted the privilege of knowing another's soul, a privilege previously belonging to friends, spouses and spiritual directors. Yet even where there seems to be so little definition, so little that can be taken for granted, we are faced with the persistent questions about the nature of our relationships and the ordering of our loves. St. Augustine's concerns about rightly ordered loves, and about their relationship to our life in

God are as relevant to us as they were to Augustine in the fifth century and to Karl Barth a generation ago.

It is perhaps inescapable that the word "friend" will be used to describe any number of relationships, ranging from casual acquaintances to the most intimate companions. We are limited by a vocabulary that inadequately expresses the nuances of complex human relations. There is no word that describes friendships of the first two sorts Aristotle described, friendships based on utility or pleasure. And we are uncomfortable with terminology like "perfect friendship" to describe Aristotle's third type based on virtue because it seems to imply a perfection none of us are capable of. We must assume, therefore, that each of us has friendships based on Aristotle's three types and that we have more of the first two sorts than of the latter one. I suspect we would agree with Cicero that friendship is not something we choose to do without. Most of us know that yearning of the soul at some time in our lives, when we long to be with that friend who knows and loves every fiber of our being, or when we have desired to have such a friend. We do not choose the loneliness and despair that feeling friendless engenders. We begin with the assumption, then, that friendship of Aristotle's most perfect sort is something that each of us desires and pursues.

This assumption then leads to the question of whether or not women and men can be friends with one another, and if so, are there any limitations on such friendships? Using Aristotle's scheme we can immediately say that friendships based on pleasure or utility are both possible and common between members of the opposite sex. Which of us does not have friends of the opposite sex who have been "useful" in helping us with some necessary task that requires strength or ability we do not have, or friends who are simply fun and enjoyable to be with; friends with whom we see films, hike, or spend time for sheer enjoyment? It is friendships of the third sort that require some thoughtful consideration.

According to Aristotle, "perfect friendships" exist between those who are similar with respect to virtue. They assume a certain quality of character on the part of each person. Such friends are also carefully chosen and limited in number. There is certainly no question about the possibility of men and women forming friendships on the bases of shared virtue, and careful and preferential choice. The major barrier to forming such friendships in the past was the requirement for equality. In the sociological contexts within which friendships were formed, men and women were not equal. Neither did they inhabit the same arenas of politics, commerce or leisure, which are three places for initiating, forming and maintaining friendships. In the monastic tradition there may well have been a greater perception of equality between the sexes than existed either in the culture or in parish churches, but the lives of those monastics were nevertheless separated by the cloister, vows and propriety. Friendships between women and men have been possible only in those times or circumstances where equality has been assumed.

We dare not, however, fall prey to two faulty assumptions: first, that women and men have in fact achieved the necessary degree of equality; second, that equality is synonymous with "sameness" or that it eliminates any differences between the sexes. "Perfect friendships" between women and men are possible only insofar as they are equal. There is, in both the culture and the church, a fairly consistent affirmation of the equality of the sexes. But the rhetoric and the reality have yet to merge in either context. Whether or not there ought to be a legislated "Equal Rights Amendment" may well be disputed, but the concerns of such an amendment's advocates cannot be: women do not receive equal pay for equal work; there are still careers from which women are effectively barred; sexual discrimination and harassment persist. What equality means theologically for the church is still at the center of discussion and debate. At the start of the 1988 Lambeth Conference a *New York Times* headline read, "To Anglicans, War of Sexes is Still Lively." The question under debate was the ordination of women to the priesthood and the episcopate, where theological affirmations of equality conflict with other affirmations and concerns.

I am not suggesting that "equality" become the sole or primary basis for making ecclesial or theological decisions; I am simply noting that, as has often been the case in both church and society, there is a gap between what we say and what we do. It is precisely that disjunction between theory and practice which makes friendships between men and women problematic, though certainly not impossible. Thankfully we need not wait for there to be full and actual equality between the sexes for such friendships to be possible. What is required is that the persons involved see one another as equal: there can be no condescension, no sense of superiority or inferiority. And it goes without saying that the other elements of friendship must be present: loyalty, mutuality, and fidelity.

Once equality has been recognized and is made the basis of friendship, we must be careful not to confuse equality with sameness. It is erroneous to claim that there is no difference between men and women, that we are all just the same. Because the differences between the sexes have been interpreted in harmful ways to *both* women and men, in ways that have perpetuated inequality, the temptation has been to deny any difference and to say that because we are the same, we ought to be equal. It is our humanity, and not our similarity, that determines equality.

In "Two Sexes" Ann Ulanov reminds us that the differentiation between the sexes is a fundamental intention of the God who made us as men and women. There are certainly ways in which we *are* the same, but equally important is the fact that we are different. It is this differentiation, together with the similarities, which most essentially reflects the image of God. It is the differentiation that carries the creative potential to "beget," to bring forth new life. It is the differentiation that teaches us love of the "other," of the one who is *not* like us, but who bears the image and grace of God. As Ann Ulanov says, it is this other who calls us out of ourselves into relation with one who is both like and unlike us.

This differentiation creates another problem for friendship. Aristotle said that a friend was essentially another self, which is true for friends of the same sex in a way not so for friends of the opposite sex. The differentiation of the sexes always implies that there is an otherness in contrasexual relations that is never eliminated. There is always some degree to which the sexes perceive the world and each other in a different way. There are some points at which the experiences of the two can never correspond. As a woman I will never fully know what it is like to be acculturated with certain expectations about career, family, and body image. I will never experience erection, ejaculation or impotence. In the same way, men will never experience other cultural expectations that are uniquely attached to the feminine, nor will they experience menstruation, child birth or menopause.

I am certainly not suggesting that friends ever have identical experiences or see the world in exactly the same way. Emerson said that friends are needed to envision and value the same truth. We each come to that truth in very different ways, but there is some point at which the experience must converge. Nevertheless, for a friend to be another self does imply a similarity of being, experience *and* perception which is more possible for friends of the same sex than it is for those of the opposite sex. Testing a friendship, of which Cicero and Plutarch both spoke, often involves telling the stories that are central to who each person is. More often than not those stories will elicit an "Ah hah!" from the other, a recognition that there is between these people a bond that already exists by virtue of some shared experience and perceptions about life and the world. Here is someone who might be entrusted with my deepest self, with knowledge of my soul.

Such differentiation does not pose an insurmountable barrier to friendship, but it does mean that there *is* a difference between friendships among members of the same sex and members of the opposite sex. I do not love my closest man-friend any less than I love my closest woman-friend. But it is true that for all our differences, my woman-friend is closer to being another self, as described by Aristotle, than is my man-friend. We have never had to be guarded with each other because of sexual hopes or expectations attached to our relationship. We have been able to share dimensions of our vocational and sexual lives that are unique to us simply because we are women. Even though we are separated by time and distance, there continues to be for us "Ah hah's" about faith and life that are not disconnected from our gender. We are by no means clones, but she is clearly my other self in the realm of the soul.

V

Even though "friend" has become a euphemism for "lover" in the past two decades, it is essential to maintain the distinction between friend and lover. As I said earlier, because of the intimacy of friendship, friends have often been assumed to be lovers. For heterosexual men and women it may be more difficult to build such an intimate relationship without crossing the line into a sexual involvement. Or strain may be put on the relationship because one of the two friends would like to have something else "happen" between them and be painfully confronted by the other's disinterest. The same can certainly happen between friends of the same sex, particularly if one is gay and the other straight. Friendship and sexual relations each have a unitive dimension, but the unity sought is different. Friends seek to become united in soul, but not exclusively with one another. Lovers, on the other hand, seek to become united in their flesh, and exclusively with the other. Friendships are exclusive only in terms of being limited in number; sexual relations are exclusive to the lover alone.

As soon as friendship crosses the line, as it were, it becomes a different relationship by a different name. And it is a line that can never again be crossed and have the friendship restored to its original state. When friends decide no longer to be lovers, the friendship has been permanently altered. There is a new caution and distance that did not exist before. In some instances there may be a sense of betrayed loyalty or fidelity. Whatever the circumstances, however, there has been a permutation of the friendship.

In *Sexual Desire: A Moral Philosophy of the Erotic*, Roger Scruton contends that "the initial aim of [sexual] desire is physical contact with the other, of the kind which is the object and the cause of arousal. No such quest for arousal enters into normal friendship or into the tender affection towards a child, even when these are focused on the embodiment of the object."[14] In other words, union with the other is the aim of sexual desire.

It is precisely at this point that friendship and sexual relationships are differentiated. In the Judeo-Christian tradition, "a man leaves his father and his mother and cleaves to his wife, and they become one flesh" (Gen. 2:24). "They are no longer two but one" (Mk. 10:8). The mystery of the marriage bond is that two become one flesh, while remaining two. The mystery of friendship is that two souls unite, while the two remain distinctly two. There is a unitive dimension in both friendship and marriage, but it is very different in each case. Husbands and wives become one flesh, and may or may not have their souls unite. The souls of friends unite, but they do not become one flesh without the relationship's primary definition changing. If friends become lovers, hopefully they do not cease being friends but the relationship acquires a different definition with a different set of moral obligations, duties, and expectations.

In "The Limits of Permissiveness", Barry Ulanov reminds us that the duties of marriage are "good cheer, mutual solace and the begetting of children." Good cheer and mutual solace may be among the obligations of friendship, but not the begetting of children. The basis for the permanence of the two relationships is also different. Friendship's permanence is based on loyalty, fidelity *and* on character. Aristotle maintained that friendships lasted as long as the friends were good. The marriage bond, in contrast, is expected to be a life-long bond. Its permanence is based on a vow made before God and witnessed by a community. There is no assumption made that a marriage will last only as long as the partners are good, even though provision has been made in Judaism and in Christianity for divorce. Within Christianity, even such provisions, however, assumed a permanence of the relationship which prohibited remarriage.

Friendship and the love between wives and husbands are not, then, synonymous loves. The primary distinction lies in the unitive dimension: those who are married become one flesh; those who are friends do not. They are also distinguished by such additional elements as the bases of permanence, different (even if sometimes corresponding) duties and obligations, different expectations for exclusiveness, and different requirements for fidelity. The latter two are connected: "perfect" friendships may be rare, but there is no expectation that they be restricted to one friend only. Having more than one friend assumes no infidelity. In contrast, marriage assumes that there is only one sexual partner and any deviation from that is an infidelity. Helen Oppenheimer is not incorrect in suggesting that good marriages either develop from or into friendship. But friendship is not the only ingredient to such a marriage, nor are the two interchangeable loves. We may well marry our best friend, but (one hopes) only after the love of friendship has been transformed to desire for the other. Roger Scruton argues that desire is eventually replaced by love which is no longer erotic, but based in trust and companionship.[15] One would hope that the erotic dimension is not actually replaced, but that trust and companionship become the glue which binds the couple. There is not a progression from friendship to erotic love and then back to friendship. Again, we are confronted with the limitations imposed on us by language. How do we discuss a friendship that is no longer friendship, per se, because the two have become lovers, and yet most of the elements of friendship are still present in the relationship? Or how do we discuss a relationship that was kindled by a flame of passion and in the course of time builds bonds of friendship? Perhaps a "good marriage," like a "perfect friendship," necessarily includes some non-negotiable elements in its definition, many of which are those same elements implicit in friendship.

I am reminded of an elderly aunt and uncle of mine who were married until parted by death in their nineties. During their last decade of life together each would frequently say that they hoped the other would die first, so that they might have a few years of peace. Their marriage was notable for its longevity and its animosity. There was little cheer, less mutual solace, and no children. It was not what one would consider a "good marriage," with no obvious element of friendship. And yet when my aunt died before my uncle, he was absolutely distraught and quite literally died of a broken heart soon after. Scruton rightly observes that there may well be love without friendship and so there was for these two.[16] Theirs might not have been a good marriage, but it *was* a marriage— with some love, some companionship, and considerable fidelity to its permanence.

It would be a mistake, therefore, to assume a correspondence between marriage and friendship which makes the two interchangeable and thereby diminishes the unique value of each. Friendship and marriage are two kinds of love with numerous points of convergence. It is not false to have or want these two kind of love: one a friendship, the other an erotic and sexual love. What is false is to think that only one kind of love is necessary or commendable. The demands of careers, families, and so on may prevent us from giving the time necessary for the sufficient development of friendship. But to say we don't need the love of friendship, that we don't need "another self," is to isolate ourselves and to deny ourselves an opportunity to learn and practice love. For those who are married to say they do not need the love of friendship may well place too great a burden and undue stress on the marital relationship. It is impossible for one other person alone to be friend, lover, companion, soul mate, and confidante. Friends are also able to see and say truths about our lives that spouses cannot, either because of their proximity to their spouse or because of the differentiation of the sexes.

It is impossible to love as God has loved us and to love as we have been commanded if we have not loved the ones closest to us. Friendship and marriage are two schools of charity, only one of which—friendship—is possible and necessary for all. We can choose to do without marriage, and there are those who are called to serve God as single people. But a life without friends is no one's destiny, no one's vocation. It is not good that any of us should be alone. We have been baptized into the church, into the community of the faithful, into the family of God. In that respect none of us are isolated and alone. But even within that community there is a longing for intimacy; a desire to be known by and to know another. Friendship provides that intimacy, that opportunity to love and be loved, to know and be known.

VI

There is one final distinction between friendship, love and marriage which must be mentioned and maintained: each is paradigmatic of a different aspect of our relationship with God.

Marriage is primarily an emblem of the relationship between God and Israel, between God and the soul, and between Christ and the church. The author of the Epistle to the Ephesians speaks of the uniting of man and woman into one flesh as a profound mystery which refers to Christ and the church (Eph. 5:32). Mystery is referred to mystery in attempting to capture the essence of the relationship.

Friendship is paradigmatic both of our friendship with God and of the Trinity. In the beginning *adam* was created in fellowship with God. In Genesis 3:8 there is an account of the "Lord God walking in the garden in the cool of the day." This image of God in search of his friends is shattered by the reality of the Fall: the man and woman are hiding themselves in shame, trying to hide their nakedness. The fellowship with God was broken by *adam*'s disobedience; it was restored by the life, death and resurrection of Jesus Christ. Friendship becomes a metaphor for describing our reconciliation with God in Christ. In John 15:14-16, Jesus says, "You are my friends if you do what I command you. No longer do I call you servants ... but I have called you friends, for all that I have heard from my Father I have made known to you." Friendship also becomes the metaphor for the kingdom of heaven, for that heavenly city where women and men neither marry or are given in marriage, but where we are friends with God and with one another. The marriage metaphor does not vanish, since the church remains the Bride of Christ. The church is the Bride of Christ and her members are friends of God's. Marriage and friendship remain two distinct relationships, in this world and in the next.

Both marriage and friendship are metaphors for understanding the Trinity. St. Thomas Aquinas said the Trinity is described in terms of friendship with God. He claimed that true happiness is impossible without joy, and that joy has its primary source in friendship. Therefore, Thomas concludes, God's true happiness requires a trinity of persons, "for with perfect friendship the lover wills that what he loves should also be equally loved by another."[17] The Trinity is a trinity of friends.

In the portrait of friendship I painted earlier, we saw that reciprocity and generosity were essential to friendship. The friend freely and generously gives to the other, and that generosity is reciprocated to some degree. "Perfect friendship" involves self-bestowal and self-expenditure by both friends. Such self-bestowal and self-expenditure are also fundamental to the inner life of God and the Trinity. God the Father gives all things to God the Son, who in turn gives all things back again through the Holy Spirit. The Incarnation is essentially about gift-giving: God gives his Son out of love, who in turn gives us life by means of giving up his life, thereby returning us to a state of friendship with God, and we in turn give our love, our praise, and our lives. We can best understand the mystery of the Trinity, of the inner life of God, and of our life in God through that relationship known and experienced as friendship. We can best understand the nature of the relationship between Christ and his church by means of the marriage bond. If we allow distinctions between these two loves to blur, then we cannnot adequately understand the mystery of our faith. Any adaptations in defining either friendship or sexual love must be carefully made, recognizing that there is more at stake than a particular relationship. The very nature of God is inextricably bound to these relationships. If fidelity in marriage becomes inconsequential, then the fidelity of Christ to the church follows suit. If friendship is reduced to a lowest common denominator and becomes little more than an acquaintance, then our friendship with God becomes equally casual and without obligation.

In the Book of Common Prayer, sacraments are called the "outward and visible signs of inward and spiritual grace, given by Christ as sure and certain means by which we receive that grace." They "sustain our present hope and anticipate its future fulfillment." These two loves are such sacraments: visible signs given by Christ, as means of grace, for the sustenance of hope.

THE LIMITS OF PERMISSIVENESS

Barry Ulanov

If you destroy in humanity its belief in immortality, every living force that sustains the life of the world would immediately be dried up. So reasons Ivan Karamazov. Nothing then would be immoral. Everything would be permissible, even cannibalism. The argument as presented in Dostoevsky's *The Brothers Kamarazov* is justly famous.[1] The prophetic Russian writer defines the terms for us today, we who have reached the point, if not of absolute destruction of our belief in immortality, then of something close enough to it. What is or is not permitted? And who does or does not do the permitting?

No bishop perhaps has yet endorsed the absolute extremes of sexual behavior, but it is not beyond the bounds of possibility to imagine an enthusiastic prelate rushing to proclaim the joys of sado-masochism as he welcomes a distinguished practitioner of that sexual devotion to his diocese. The fact is that after the tumultuous emptying of the closets and the proud proclaiming and noisy parading of belief in, and practice of, what was once defined as off-limits sexual behavior, all things are possible.[2]

We have been here before, if not precisely in this corner of Western civilization, then certainly in most of the other centers of culture and wisdom on our side of the East-West divide. There is a small difference. In the earlier courtings of young children for sexual exploration and intense research into the permutations and combinations into which appetites could be driven, the explorers and researchers did not write manifestos in defense of their work nor seek to make converts with philosophical or theological treatises.[3] Today, in our new permissiveness, and following the custom of the times, we construct elaborate apologia for our lubricity. What once might have been matter for the confessional is now a hotly defended way of life in which those who are thoughtless enough to express opposition are attacked as *phobes*, and those who are tasteless enough to practice a conventional sexuality, though without voicing any objection to the unconventional, are dismissed as *philes*.

This new way of conducting a sexual life in public deserves its own name. I propose Liberation Sexuality as appropriate in every way. I make this proposal not in order to condemn the large and varied number of performers, philosophers, and theologians who might be called Liberation Sexualists, but better to understand them and how they got to be that way. More seriously, I do so to try to make some sense of all this for those of gentle sensibility and tender conscience, however few they may be, who find themselves bewildered or affronted by Liberation Sexuality, or simply out of touch with it.

I ask the old question, consecrated by two centuries of revolutionary usage, "What is to be done?"[4] Clearly, dismissal out of hand is neither useful nor proper. Even if we do not accept the great numbers proposed for Liberation Sexuality by its most ardent adherents or its most determined opponents, we do recognize, we must recognize, that it is not an inconsequential number of people we are talking about. Nor can we fail to understand today, with so much clinical evidence thrusting itself at us, what literature and the other arts have given eloquent witness to for millennia, that human sexual need is prodigious and that in the search for its satisfaction there is nothing too devious, too extreme, too shameful. We know also, if we have looked with any thoroughness or honesty at our own sexuality or that of others, that unfulfilled or misapplied sexuality can bring terrible suffering, and that is not to speak of the physical disease, the moral destruction, the multiple ways of achieving corruption, diminution, and death that congregate around our sexual life. No, dismissal is not possible; the issues that Liberation Sexuality poses for us are issues of survival. We must take it very seriously indeed. What then is to be done?

Horrified by the suffering, we can do as Ivan Karamazov promises to do, to resign "as soon as possible" from the human urge to avenge suffering and satisfy indignation. "Too high a price is asked for harmony," he says. We simply cannot afford it. "And so I hasten to give back my entrance ticket . . . . It's not God that I don't accept . . . only I most respectfully return Him the ticket."[5]

Rebellion is the word Ivan's brother Alyosha uses to describe Ivan's attitude, and rebellion it is. What he is rebelling against is freedom. It is not harmony for which too high a price is demanded but freedom; and with freedom, love; and with love, still more freedom; and with love too, all its opposites and opponents, hate and haters, and evildoers. This is the scandal of freedom, as for so long theologians and poets have understood. This is the scandal of permissiveness.

If in God's permissive will we are free to do good, then by definition we are also free to do . But equally, if we are free to commit acts, we are also free to perform good ones. What is scandalous is that there is no absolute guarantee, no constraint upon us to be good, to do good. We are set loose in God's world, free to be whatever and whoever we will be, partakers of God's largesse, another word for which is permissiveness.

Ivan can accept God but not His world and not really His people, the people His permissiveness has allowed to be: "It's just one's neighbors, to my mind, that one can't love, though one might love those at a distance." Close up, people do terrible things, smell bad, become in a word unlovable: "For any one to love a man, he must be hidden, for as soon as he shows his face, love is gone." And so Ivan tenders his resignation, as so many others do, though rarely with the same honesty or boldness of spirit. How can one love a race—the human race— that practices a "degrading, humiliating suffering" as a matter of course, whose soldiers spear babies on their bayonets or after petting them and making them laugh point their pistols at them and blow their brains out? Can one imagine loving parents who smear a child with her own excrement as punishment, as one might housebreak a dog?[6]

The answer to this endless demeaning suffering is the harmony proposed by Ivan's—and Dostoevsky's—elegant utopian, the ninety-year-old Grand Inquisitor in the "legend" created by Ivan's imagination to deal with his terrible doubts. The paradisal demon imagined by Ivan envisions a society in which everyone's wants are satisfied, in which a small number of supermen bring peace and order to the mass of creatures, a weak and feckless race which can accept its lot happily. All that is missing is freedom and therefore love. Freedom is unendurable in the perfect society and so is its progenitor, Jesus Christ. He must be executed by the Inquisition. The logic is unanswerable. But Jesus, listening in silence to the arguments of utopian socialist orthodoxy, has an answer: "He suddenly approached the old man in silence and softly kissed him on his bloodless aged lips. That was all his answer. The old man shuddered. His lips moved." His words are few, his gesture is clear. He opens a door for Jesus and says, "Go, and come no more . . . . come not at all, never, never!"[7]

Freedom persists. Love persists. Permissiveness is everywhere. The first permits the second, the second demands the first. Free to love, loving in freedom, identifiable by our permissiveness, we often commit the most grotesque acts in the name of one or the other. We may discover that we have acted under compulsion. We may be diagnosed as obsessive, or more grandly, obsessive-compulsive. But to us, the most controlled of us or the least controlled, our acts proceed from motivations of love. The ancient diagnosis of St. Thomas Aquinas, so handsomely seconded by Richard Hooker, has not been superseded by the modern clinicians of love. We act, however we act, out of love, if only love for ourselves. When we kill, we kill with love, whether it is to remove an obstacle in our lives, to end another's pain, or to satisfy some pathology in ourselves. In our most bizarre, humiliating, and debauching sexual acts, it is love that impels us. It may be love perverted, love defective, or love excessive, but love it is. It may be love of the wrong thing, or love of the right thing in hopelessly exaggerated amounts, or a poor wispy undernourished parody of love, but to us it is love and at the moment of the act it is as love we experience it.[8]

To call sexual coupling "the act of love" is not as so many have seemed to think a resort to euphemism to avoid a once-offensive Anglo-Saxon monosyllable, or what is even more uncomfortable for some, the sterile abstractions that seem better adapted to describe farmyard matings, the behavior of linking verbs, college roommates, or political meetings, words like fornication, copulation, cohabitation, sexual congress. St. Thomas's apercu is well supported by our constant use of this phrase or the complementary "making love." It may come hard to a man or woman caught in the throes of sexual acting-out to speak of love, to bring to the physical exertions the metaphysical grace of the terse confession, "I love you," but somewhere, even in the most tortured and self-serving of sexual encounters, the sensation and therefore the language of love will manifest themselves. Beyond everything else we do, what we do sexually feels, tastes, smells of love. Something in us understands that the energies caught up or unleashed in our sexual acts spring from, or may lead to, some ultimate revelation. The mystery of the human person is somehow, no matter how paradoxically or ironically, reflected in our sexual being.

We must, to begin with, accept the physical geography of our sexuality, the fact that the seat of our digestive emptyings is also the place of our deepest bodily fulfillment. It may remain a source of shame for some, but the neighborhood in which our sexuality lives and finds its permissiveness is unmistakable. Jonathan Swift confronts the facts bluntly in his poem "The Lady's Dressing Room." His male protagonist, sorting through the "frowzy heaps" of milady's effects, gets past the "snuff and snot" of handkerchiefs and all the rest of the apparel and accoutrements of a woman's boudoir, to have finally to face the facts of her inner life, that pot where women made in Swift's time what James Joyce called their "chamber music."[9]

> Thus finishing his grand survey,
> Disgusted Strephon stole away,
> Repeating in his amorous fits,
> Oh! *Celia, Celia, Celia shits!*

The poem, as funny as it is melancholy, as wise as it is disconsolate in contemplating the facts of life, asks at the end the crucial question.

> Should I the Queen of love refuse
> Because she rose from stinking ooze?

We should not, I think, be troubled over Swift's apparent discomfort at the design of love's quarters. The architecture and landscaping are as described. The question remains. What are we to make of it? Yeats made a very great deal of it through the persona of his Crazy Jane, that splendidly resolute woman who in several poems from a seven-poem sequence and in one other work meets "the Bishop," a sour old fellow based securely enough on the ordinary of Connaught, who in Yeats' time had advised his people not to read anything that set forth the degrading passion of love. In the best of the lot, "Crazy Jane Talks with the Bishop," the old cleric, meeting Jane "on the road," has much to say, much to advise.

> ' Those breasts are flat and fallen now,
> Those veins must soon be dry;
> Live in a heavenly mansion,
> Not in some foul sty.'

Crazy Jane is not won over. Her theology is not at all upset by love's geography or the homily the Bishop draws from it. First she pronounces the general truth:

'Fair and foul are near of kin,
And fair needs foul,' I cried.

Then, after a laconic acknowledgement of her age in the loss of her friends and her contemporaries to death, she says almost as much as can be said about the fact, triumphant to her, that acts of love and excretion occupy the same territory, and that in a woman there is a sexual organ that can rise in its own small loving splendor.

'A woman can be proud and stiff
When on love intent;
But Love has pitched its mansion in
The place of excrement;
For nothing can be sole or whole
That has not been rent.'

For Crazy Jane there is no contradiction in the double life of her organs. This is the nature of woman as she understands it; this is the nature of love. In "Crazy Jane on the Day of Judgment," she proclaims the principle straightaway.

'Love is all
Unsatisfied
That cannot take the whole
Body and soul';
And that is what Jane said.[10]

Crazy Jane needs no bishop's permission, no theologian's instruction to make the right choice. Her magisterium is her own body, her own soul, from which she has learned that it is in the conflicts and contradictions of the human condition that divine resolution is to be found. The breaking of a membrane is the signal for the knitting together of the body and spirit of love. We are contrary beings. In our freedom, we must constantly discover and rediscover, as if for the first time, the meaning of that paradigm of St. Augustine's, in which through our freedom we are permitted to grow to the ultimate freedom, where we really no longer can choose to sin because nothing in our freedom moves us thus to do. The formula is simple:

posse peccare

posse non peccare

non posse peccare

We are able to sin. We are able not to sin. We are not able to sin. Of such copybook maxims is wisdom compounded and the territory of permissiveness made open to us.

These, it seems to me, are the best words available to us to face and make sense of the mystery of original sin, which is what everywhere confronts us in our permissiveness.[11] We are able to sin. We are able not to sin. With sufficient grace and our correspondence with it, we may reach the almost unimaginable state of being in which we really cannot move ourselves to sin. The temptations are endless—to goodness as much as to and they must, the good and both, be treated as temptations. That is the point of John Donne's sonnet, "Batter my heart, three person'd God."

Donne piles metaphor upon simile in his urgency to explain how much the libido we bring to God resembles the desire we think of as illicit. First, in this demanding prayerful poem, he says plaintively that God has only thus far nudged him, come up to him much too politely, really:

for, you

As yet but knocke, breathe, shine, and seeke to mend.

Not good enough. Take me up as a glass-blower might seize and break open a glass pipette to make it over into something fresh and fine and good:

That I may rise, and stand, o'erthrow mee, and bend
Your force, to breake, blowe, burn and make me new.

He tells the Lord that he is occupied, "like an usurpt towne,
to another due," that he has tried to let Him in, but without
success. Nor has the Lord's "viceroy," reason, been any help,
for reason too "is captiv'd, and proves weake or untrue." But
the desire, the overwhelming temptation to move toward God,
remains, and he the poet, John Donne, our spokesman, im-
plores the Lord again to take him, to use every contrary force
to put love in its proper place. The language is, as it must be,
voluptuous, for that is the nature of Donne's love, tutored as it
is by that central truth of human freedom and permissiveness,
that a true love, whether the object is human or divine, is at
least as combative, as sensual, as driven, as wonderfully
paradoxical as a false one.

Yet dearely I love you, and would be loved faine,
But am betroth'd unto your enemie:
divorce mee, untie, or breake that knot againe,
Take mee to you, imprison mee, for I
Except you enthrall mee, never shall be free,
Nor ever chast, except you ravish mee.[12]

Donne is writing, praying, begging, confessing, allegorizing
in a proud tradition. The recourse to the language of bodily
sexuality to translate the movement of the soul toward God is
an ancient one with august scriptural sanction in the Song of
Songs. Just before Donne's time, in sixteenth-century Spain,
perhaps the most moving examples of all these translations of
spirit into the imagery of the flesh were accomplished by an
astonishingly large number of Spanish mystics, most notably
Fray Luis de Leon, St. Teresa of Avila, and St. John of the
Cross.[13] All these worthies, as well as their remarkable four-

teenth-century predecessors in England and the Low Countries and their twelfth-century French tutelaries, give ample warning against the movements of the body which almost invariably accompany the use of such imagery. To go to God with love is to go by way of the cross, the Franciscan Bernardino de Laredo tells us. The soul that looks to go directly into this love must "try to be detached from the body as regards sensuality, for he who will lose his life here is to find it in life eternal."[14] The founders of the tradition, St. Jerome, whose translation of the Song is the source from which the richest, most effulgent love poetry springs, and the Greek fathers who make so much of the Song in their commentaries, Origen and Gregory of Nyssa, are even more stern on this account. But body and soul cannot be so easily separated. The sensuality remains. To move from love of the human flesh to love of its maker is not to drop as so much unwanted baggage the glands, muscles, nerves, and the imagination which, temperate or intemperate, fires them.[15]

We are destined to be wholes, no matter what Crazy Jane's bishop or other masters of a prurient warning-off may tell us. If we come gladly toward God, we come with body as well as spirit, and it is only enthralled, as John Donne says, that we can be free, only ravished by the Lord that we can be chaste. The permissiveness in which we live our lives of freedom and love is as large and paradoxical and enabling as all that. The Lord whose permission makes it possible for us to make our judgments of love, to act our acts of love, to conform our bodies and souls to every possible end, noble and ignoble—that Lord is a jealous God, as we are told again and again in Scripture, jealous beyond everything, it seems, to assure our freedom.

In the jealousy which so assiduously guarantees our freedom, the Lord does not cut our freedom off wherever and whenever it might interfere with our orderly progress toward purity and goodness or make us less responsive to the counsels of perfection. And so at the very least our lives founder, at least some of the time, in promiscuity and at the worst fall into tragedy.

Those are the conditions of freedom and the permissiveness which rules it and they are nowhere so unmistakable as in the sexual life. We have our exemplary lives in the tradition of nursery rhymes and beast fables where an early innocence succeeds to a later innocence and not a single voluptuary itch or sportive dream, much less a direct experience of the flesh, comes to trouble the good creatures. In our more tough-minded narratives of sexual awakening and development, starting with Scripture, the textures are different. Dreams and fantasies erupt unbidden into the wildest wanton pastures. The flesh hurts: our organs are not instructed by the consoling purity of the rhymes and fables. The imagination pierces: we are sent God alone knows where in search of appeasement and resolution.[16]

Our sexual lives are of a mixed and disorderly composition. They rarely start with a simple easy sweetness. They are often visited by deeply troubling guilts, brought to us by others, or when those are not in ready supply, by ourselves. This is the experience, if the truth be told, even of Liberation Sexualists, who have cast off all constraints and have vowed never to feel guilty again. In all this, there are always possible disturbances of the body and the mind and the soul, which must live out the consequences of a boundless freedom and can at any moment be afflicted by sexual dysfunction. The sources of the dysfunction, we all know by now, may be imaginary, but the body lamed or halted in its sexual exercise, the frightened mind, the shaken spirit are just as disturbed as if the sources were visible under microscope or x-ray.

The miracle is that love remains, not only as motivation for our worst as for our best acts, but as a way of life and one that works. There are no certain prescriptions which will bring us to it, though there are I think attitudes of mind, preparations of the soul, graces of being, which will serve to encourage the possibility of love and its nurturing growth and development when it comes. There are not many proscriptions either which will assure us of not standing in the way of love, though here, in the negative precincts of human sexuality, there are unmistakable things to be avoided, movements of the body and the imagination to be faced and acknowledged and if possible turned away from.

If we can accept the fact that we live our sexual lives as we do so much of the rest of our existence, in an atmosphere of promiscuity and tragedy, we can begin to make our way toward that state of being in which it is possible to recognize and receive and correspond with the graces of love. There is no way around it. We have choices to make and we must know what they are and how to make them. The permissiveness in which a loving sexuality flourishes or decays or just stumbles along requires a constant vigilance founded upon honesty and courage. There is no room for denial here. Once we forswear the nursery rhymes and fables of love, we must also give up the wishful fantasy that the disagreeable or at least ambiguous dreams and fantasies which come to us do not really exist. We must look at ourselves as we really are and accept ourselves as we really are.

The conventional phrase that indicates that we have really seen someone, ourself or another, is to say that we have seen that person "warts and all." The conventional phrase is wrong. We may have seen the warts, or deformities far worse to look at and take in, much less to accept cheerfully. But what we have seen is not the person, only something on the surface that may indeed affect the person but does not, no matter how severe a departure from what we think of as normal physical appearance, define the person or offer anything much more than a suggestion of what the person is by showing us what the person has to live with or without.

Nor does stripping a person naked offer much more, however entertaining, tantalizing, or even arousing the experience may be. A naked person may be a delight or a disappointment. The womanly bosom or manly chest thus revealed may inspire lovely thoughts and what follows, from waist to toes, front and back, may add its own delicious tremors, a feast to the eye and a positive banquet for the imagination. On the other hand, the eye may be shocked by the body thus confronted and the imagination terribly let down. Without benefit of support and cosmetic, the person—the outer person, the surface person—may be so much less or more than what had been expected, that the whole experience suffers. But pleasant or unpleasant, depressing or even thrilling, it is not an experience of a whole person and we must remember that.

It is not easy to do so. If a body does not measure up to our expectations, or worse, on close inspection reveals all sorts of deficiencies as the world measures these things, that may make any attempt to find something beyond the surface just too difficult. We have expectations, and they are not too unreasonable after all, are they? No, he or she won't do. Sorry. Just too much of this or too little of that. Ugh.

The opposite experience is not necessarily more enlightening or dependable. We may feel elated to have found just what we have been looking for, perfect measurements, marvelous proportions, the ideal body for our tastes. Splendid, especially if the perfect anatomy is supported by a matching perfection in sexual performance. But still, with all that new delight, all that new arousal in intimate exchanges, we may not yet have met the whole person, though we may have come a little closer to it.

This is where pornography does its dirty little business. Pornography? That "literature" of sexuality unfettered (or in chains, if you prefer) and endlessly pleasurable, and the photography that makes it clear? Yes, pornography, for what pornography is about is surfaces, and surfaces alone. If the surfaces lack this or that or have a bit too much here and there, then there are always airbrushes to make things right. The finished photograph proves that perfection exists in the body, and photographs, people would like to believe, do not lie. But of course photographs do lie, and the pornographic picture, still or moving, almost always does lie. So does what might be called "airbrush literature." In pornographic stories, endowments are always impeccable and energies without limit or cost. All men are willing; that is a universal given, as it has been for millennia. More and more women are equally willing or even more than equally compliant or predatory. The shy and demure, the frigid, and the frightened personae of all those dramas of the fate worse than death have all but disappeared, as a whole new scholarship of women's undercover late-night "romantic" reading is only too happy to inform us.[17] Came the pill and went the romance. The old frustration was that they never got the "good parts." The new frustration is that that is all there is.

It does not matter whether magazines or films or novels are easily recognizable as pornographic or even self-proclaimed to be. If the action is confined to surfaces, the effect is almost sure to be pornographic. There is no room for the person. People are abstracted—breasts and chests, legs and arms, rumps and genitals—like so many props and fixtures in a robot sexual drama. All that is missing is the concrete person, the whole person.[18]

How can one condemn such abstractions? They are not grossly indecent, repulsive, loathsome. They are in fact quite the opposite much of the time—sleek, handsomely photographed, joyful people having a wonderful time in just the sort of place most of us would think to describe with those words on a tourist postcard. And yet they are, I think, obscene. They belittle the human person even as they enlarge it. They rob it of its particular identity, and never more so than when they reduce sexual exchanges to measurement, athleticism, and staying power. The most profound reach of a loving sexuality, into contemplation of the individual person, is not even broached, and thus the special strengths and wisdom of human sexuality are altogether missed.

Everything about human sexuality—its order and disorder, its frustrations and completions, its most demeaning experiences, its most fulfilling moments—can be directed to a greater understanding of the human person and in it can be found confirmation of the worth of that person, even the one least fulfilled or most demeaned by a particular experience. The strippings and revealings of sexual experience, if they are not confined to surfaces, permit us to see just what inside us moves us or does not move us to bodily response. We do so not to chart physiological responses, glandular activity, a movement of muscle or nerve, but rather to discover what depths of spirit may find outlet in our animal functions. We do not do this as observing scholars, standing aside from our sexual activity even as we engage in it, but rather somehow in these most intimate exchanges come to know ourselves better and even more come to know the other and to identify what in him or her really is other. Comparative measurements are not in it, though obviously both of us in a sexual meeting are of a particular size and shape. What we have stretched before us or wrapped in and around us is much more than a body. It is a person, which is to say, in Boethius's crunchy Latin, *naturae rationabilis individua substantia*, a self-subsisting individual of rational nature.[19]

What a person meant to Boethius in the sixth century, and should continue to mean to us today, is an individual complete in himself or herself, not "accidental" to any subject, not a chance happening, but a rational being existing for herself or himself. No matter how caught up we may be in the jubilant rituals of sexuality, we are there as rational individuals. The touches we share, the feelings we excite or that are aroused in us, the exchanges of juices in which we may for a moment lose consciousness—none of this reduces either our rationality or individuality, or at least should not, if we want to get the most out of the experience. We are not farm animals breeding or being bred to satisfy our owners. We own ourselves. We come with senses, judgment, understanding, all the resources of our rational nature, even if we choose for a time to suspend the conscious operation of one or another of these extraordinary powers. Something in us somewhere will register what we have been doing and with whom, and will give us a new insight into the doers as well as the doing, or at least can do so if we make ourselves open to our apparatus of insight, our individual rational nature, our equipment and identity as human persons. What is more, we will discover, if we look for it, that we have a whole encyclopedia of such insights within us that, with whatever degree of consciousness or unconsciousness, we have been compiling for years.

One of the remarkable facts about our sexual life is that we remember so much of it, and in such great detail. We remember what we have done with elegance; we remember where we have been clumsy or inept or just downright boring. Somewhere in us there is a meticulous record of those with whom we have had sexual relations, earth-moving, as Hemingway once put it, or trivial, or just haplessly furtive. Books have been written about first sexual experiences and there is a vast literature—sociological, anthropological, psychological—that persists in calling these introductions to the territory "initiation rites" or "fertility rites." The significance of these moments may have been exaggerated but not their persistence in our memories.

Our sexual meetings stay with us because clearly they are more than mere social engagements or the commonplace product of our newly liberated lives. Even professionals in the game are said to retain a more than blurred record of their encounters, particularly those they would rather forget. The point is, whether we remember with pleasure or embarrassment, blow by blow or with just a generalized sense of what happened, we hold on to these moments in our lives because they remind us of something central to us as persons. There were in these comings together, there always will be in them, the seeds of relationship. The seeds may not have grown. The relationship, if such it was, may have collapsed. But relationships are what it is about and that central agency in us which takes note of these things keeps a full account of them.

We do well to reconnoiter the territory. What we find, if we suppress the denials which so often accompany these forays into our sexual history, is that we are not by intention creatures of surfaces no matter how often we may have succumbed to surface allurements. We want relationship, all of us. We want to know others. We want others to know us. We want the support, the gathering in, that tells us we are persons and worthy of the interest of other persons,[20] that our lives are worth sharing, that we may even be lovable to someone somewhere.

I am not talking now about the dreams of romance, our hope for a fairy-tale Prince or Princess Charming who will wake us from our long dreary sleeping lives, though there is nothing wrong in some larger-than-life textures coloring our expectations as long as we do not demand that every sexual event have heroic dimension.[21] The center of my concern here is that we know where we have been, that we know what we can be sexually. Relationship beckons. Sexuality demands it. Our personhood cannot survive long without it. Our moment on earth will be defined by it.

We must prepare ourselves for relationship. That is what the theology of procreation is about *au fond*, the begetting of relationships. To bring new being into the world is not simply a matter of producing children nor of coming together in that brief embrace that assures insemination. The science of genetics has demonstrated with chilling precision how many ways there are to generate children that do not require any human meeting. Liberation Sexuality, furthermore, encourages the belief that not only will ectogenesis, the gestation of the fetus outside the womb, become commonplace, but also parthenogenesis, women producing children without any male assistance. Can the situation in *Aucassin and Nicolete* of the King of Torelore, who bears the children while his Queen leads their soldiers in battle, be far behind?[22]

A true relationship begets new being, a mixing of persons, a coupling of persons, which in itself is a whole new order of persons. Here is our most considerable strengthening against fear and uncertainty and bewilderment, even against the terrors and debilitations of extreme poverty and physical suffering. We survive against all odds with the community of relationship, which grows from, which depends upon, which survives only because of, two people coming together. Thus it is that twice in Deuteronomy (20: 5-7; 24:5) it states that a newly married man shall have a year free of war, or "any business" that might be "charged" him, to spend with his wife. In the first of these passages, the ritual has its firm logic: "What man is there that hath built a new house, and hath not dedicated it . . . . And what man is he that hath planted a new vineyard, and hath not yet eaten of it? And what man is there that hath betrothed a wife, and hath not taken her?" In each case, the threat is that another may take the fruits of the man's work if he dies in battle—his house, his vineyard, his wife—and he not benefit at all. Let him dedicate his house, eat of his vineyard, take his wife to him, and then after a year of these fruits go off to war.[23]

The second passage speaks even more directly to the community of marriage and what its being identifies and commands. "When a man hath taken a new wife ... he shall be free at home one year, and shall cheer up his wife which he has taken." Good cheer, mutual solace, these are as much the duties and functions of the marital community as producing a child. In the wisdom of our ancient progenitors, we are seen as coming together to create being in many ways. All involve relationship for all come from the meeting of persons, and persons do not define themselves by a simple farmyard husbandry, calving or yeaning to preserve the species.

In the permissiveness which gives us dominion over the animals, we must with all due unsentimental regard for them separate ourselves from them. We can rut like animals, we can pop our young from our wombs like animals, we can go mindlessly about our sexual tasks in the same way that our survival requires us to feed ourselves with whatever is at hand if we have gone too long without carefully prepared and appetizing food. But there is little satisfaction that way, as the endless testimony of the Don Juans and other less celebrated lechers of the world suggests, for what their narratives insist upon more than anything else is a failure of appeasement, an impotence of the person if not of the prostate gland to find fulfillment. Leporello's great comic catalogue of the Don's seductions in Mozart's and Da Ponte's *Don Giovanni* tells us how ceaselessly, how tonelessly, how much without a sense of the person, his own or his woman's, how much like a raging bull he goes about his seductions.

This is the catalogue of the women my master has loved . . . . look at it, read it with me. In Italy, 640; in Germany, 231; one hundred in France, 91 in Turkey, but, in Spain, 1,003! Among them, countrywomen, chambermaids, city ladies; countesses, baronesses, marchionesses, princesses, women of every class, every shape, every age. In blondes, he praises gentility; in brunettes, fidelity; in white-haired old women, tenderness. In winter, he looks for plumpness; in summer, thinness, tallness, majesty. In little women, he always finds charm. He conquers the old just to add them to his list. But his great passion is for the young beginner—doesn't matter whether she's rich or ugly or beautiful, as long as she wears a skirt. You know what he's like!

And that is the peak achievement of a sexuality without persons, a sexuality of surfaces, a sexuality of endless permissiveness and altogether without recollection except the numbers of those who have been trampled in the lust, with perhaps a nod here and there to identify them in groups by nation, color, class, size, or age. Imagine how much less there is in the game for the two-dimensional Don Juans of everyday life, those without the words of a Da Ponte or the music of a Mozart to translate their swollen appetites and minuscule fulfillments into the dimensions of operatic fable.[24]

The identifying characteristic of our Don Juans, apart from their inability to achieve satisfaction, sexual or any other kind, is their reduction of their encounters to part-objects.[25] They not only look at their partners as representatives of the kind of group Leporello identifies so well, denominated by country or caste or shape or age, but as examples of out-sized parts. The Don Juan of the corner drugstore or the fast-food emporium fits his vocabulary to his vision; he speaks to us in his noble rhetoric of love as a "tits" man or an "ass" or "leg" fancier. His female equivalent attains her peak of eloquence with the all-embracing superlative "What a hunk!" In the reductionist sexual economics of Don Juanism and its part-object exchanges, there is no room for relationship or the ethics of being that both the restrictiveness of relationship and its latitude foster.

In relationship we do in fact discover both the particular limits of God's permissiveness and its endless wide-open possibilities. Everything about human experience supports that interpretation. Reason tells us as much. Revelation insists upon it. All the injunctions of Scripture point to that reading. We are enjoined against coveting another being, which is to say we must not be avaricious about what belongs to someone else, especially that most important belonging of all, his or her person. If it is not betrothed to another, in or out of wedlock, then at the very least it is his or her own being, own belonging, and is not to be grasped at or grabbed in a kind of mindless concupiscence, even when everything seems to encourage the grasping and grabbing, not the least the grabbee's evident eagerness. The coveting which is in itself adulterous is the one that falsifies our persons, that brings us together mechanically, without imagination, without grace.

So it is too with the other sexual indulgences that revelation mocks or condemns. It is not a matter of reducing sodomy or onanism to a particular act. Both are held in scriptural contempt because as understood, in context, they reflect a disregard of persons. The opposite procedure, in which scrupulous measurements of the sexually permissible are kept in copious detail, in books of moral theology or in such parodies of a Christian sexual ethic as Hollywood's Legion of Decency rules, is itself a form of adultery or sodomy or onanism. This sort of spelling out, in precise anatomical and physiological detail, of where and how virtuous and thus allowable sexual activity becomes sinful and thus impermissible, is insulting to the human person. It betrays it by assuming it has exact measurements to its passions, that a millimeter more breast shown in a film close-up, a sheet permitted to fall just another inch, a certain kind of moving round in a bed, against a wall, wherever, and all the pent-up sexual energy of audiences will erupt. This is to make unnatural connections, which is the sin of sodomy. This is sexual incompletion, which is the sin of onanism. This is that traducing of the permissiveness in which we live our freedom for which the proper name is adultery.

In sexual relationships our majestic possibility is to find our persons.[26] None of this can be held to easily statable rule or procedure. We are in a world of mystery. We can penetrate it. We can go more and more deeply into it. We can never exhaust it, never come out at its other end, as through some discoverable geography. We correspond with its graces in symbolic enactments, the sexual exchanges which love demands but does not specify and never makes final. There is no more a finished list of what a loving sexuality permits than there is a revelation or a logic that identifies what love can never tolerate. All that we know is that the purpose of love, that the accomplishment of its symbolic sexual enactments, is the disclosing of the human person. That is enough.

We know it is enough, and yet the scandal of freedom remains. We would like our permissiveness to be contained within specific boundaries. Do this but not that. These holds, these falls are licit in the wrestling maneuvers of love. These grabs and grunts and blows beneath the waist are distinct fouls; they are unmistakably out of bounds. And then before we know it the measurements are back. "Bless me, Father, for I have sinned. It has been eight weeks since my last confession. In that time I have been guilty of four orals, three genitals, and one demi-anal—sort of."

Is that the way we come together? Is any meeting of persons possible with that sort of moral arithmetic? Is the opposite any better? You may have all the joys of what the greatest of medieval sexual satirists, Andreas Capellanus, called "pure love." You may hug and kiss and nibble and pummel and do all of this naked, but without the "final solace." In other words, you may work at extended teasing, a sort of delicate, taunting sadism blessed by the church.[27]

Ah, but the church would never do that, would it? But of course it would, and has, and will do so again if we insist on literal-minded moral simplifications as a way of dealing with the temptations of freedom. What our permissive state demands is something quite different, a willingness to expose our persons, a determination to look as unembarrasedly as possible on the other person. That is what we should strip and be stripped to reveal—the naked ego.

The naked ego is the person revealed, revealed not only to other persons but to itself. This is the way we achieve presence, by giving to what is most alive in ourselves the freedom to make all its claims. Those claims are both of the body and of the soul, of the senses and of the reason. They may enlarge us; they may diminish us. The essential truth about these claims of the ego is their insistence upon bringing flesh and spirit together, and not only this moment's flesh and spirit, but the flesh we have inhabited in the past and the spirit that in the past has inhabited us, and the flesh and spirit that we may become in the future. The German theologian Eberhard Jungel puts it very well, losing none of the nuances of being or time in his exposition of the effects of the "nearness of the ego to itself" which being "addressed about God" induces in us.

> Spiritual presence is the most original capacity of the ego, to be fully present through the surpassing of the state of being-here which is identical with the state of being-now. This capacity is the unique characteristic of the ego as a *zoon*

logon echon ("living being have the word, or speech").
Spiritual presence would be falsely understood if one sought
to understand it as the opposite concept to the sensual
presence of the ego. In contrast to such a spiritualizing or
intellectualizing view, spiritual presence is rather to be understood as the ego's state of being present in its entire
sensuality. In its sensuality as a body, the ego is here now,
whereas as spirit it draws this its sensual state of being here
through distancing into the past and the future and qualifies
it thus as the present. This present which is always coming
to itself out of the past and the future could be called the
continuity of the human ego.[28]

In that continuity of the ego we find ourselves, and, it must
be repeated, we find what we are, what we have been, what we
may be. We meet ourselves, we meet the *I* which is nobody
else's but ours alone, no matter in how many ways others may
seem to be the same, to look the same, to act as we do. We meet
others, other *I*'s, each completely his or her own *I*, each in
some way or ways his or her own person, again, no matter how
much he or she may seem no more than a type, a member of
a class, a cliche among humans stamped from an all-too-
familiar mold.

Meeting *I* to *I* is the most strenuous of experiences. It is
also the most consoling, or at least can be. For when we allow
the ego to make its claims in our most intimate encounters, we
find ourselves emerging as persons, and we discover how
much that encourages others to show themselves for what they
are, to be their own person. We come then in our intimacy to
know each other and discover beyond argument that that
knowing is the most precious of the results of our sexual
coming together, not the number of free falls, or even of
damnable but delightful illicit twists and turns. We know now
why the Bible's use of the verb "to know," as in "to know each
other," is the most appropriate of all possibilities to describe

sexual encounter and far from being a euphemism is much more to the point than any of the explosive monosyllables or overloaded circumlocutionary phrases commonly used to describe human sexual experience.[29]

When we know each other sexually, symbolically, freely, know each other as persons, we know relationship. We have met in the body. We have met in the spirit. We have deepened and enlarged our being. We have encountered, with some degree of awareness, being itself. Our vocabularies may not be equipped for this kind of language. We may feel shy or embarrassed at even trying to think this way. How can such a rollicking, robust physical experience in any way be said to have embraced the metaphysical? But it has. This meeting of persons, this sort of knowing sexual meeting, is a kind of prayer.

It may be bold to think this way about our sexuality, but it is not inflated or pretentious, and the boldness is the boldness of the children of light. In our freedom as sexual beings we achieve relationship. In relationship, we do not act out so much as we act in. We move more and more deeply inside ourselves, knowing him, knowing her, knowing each other, knowing personhood, knowing being to what seems like the fullest of our capacities. In so doing we come to the source of our being, to what makes being possible. We come to that direct experience of the good which is one of the two ways that best defines a loving relationship, I think. The other is to see in it and know through it one of the most satisfactory of the distillations into human terms of the mystery of being which Christians know and worship as the Trinity.

The limits of permissiveness are reached this way, if I may for a moment play on the words. Anything that impedes our reaching these limits is wrong, wrong for us even if not intrinsically wrong, and to be avoided or altogether banished from our lives. It may be a sexual practice, a habit of the imagination, even something as seemingly trivial as a particular set of words or gestures. If it reduces rather than enhances being, if it keeps us from meeting persons as persons, it limits us grievously, it is unacceptable. On the other hand, whatever spiritualizes the flesh and fleshifies the spirit is limited only by our ability to recognize what is coming toward us, to take it and rejoice in it. The limitation here is in what an older language of the spiritual life calls "the discernment of spirits." Not everyone has this gift at the apogee, but there is a kind of democracy at work here in the fact that in the sexual life every human being, at some level of understanding, is endowed with the ability to approach or be approached with grace by another human being. This is the sacramentality of sexual intimacy, in which every shadow reveals in one way or another something of the substance which in its human or divine form we call by the name of person.

These are the bounds of the Christian sexual ethic. We grow as persons to know persons. The urge to do so is in all of us and the desire to understand it and experience it in sexual acts invariably accompanies the urge. In our movements toward growth as sexual persons, as human persons, we are sometimes clumsy, often disordered, uncertain as to our motivation, insecure about our yearnings, badly connected between body and spirit, and almost always at a loss as to how to effect the connection. We are promiscuous in our sexual behavior. We sin. It is not much help then simply to identify our failures and to call down imprecations on our head for them. We need instruction, we need prayer at least as much as we need condoms or drilling in the sexual habits of humankind accompanied by film demonstration or live act. The call to arms—and the rest of the body—by Liberation Sexuality does not help here. That way lies only a kind of meaningless self-indulgence and soon enough very little gratification of any kind, a fact to which the back wards of hospitals and asylums and the front rooms of therapists constantly testify. We seem to have to learn over and over again, and tragically, the folly of the doctrine of "safe sex." It is not a bad lesson to learn, for all its tragic textures, if it helps to concentrate our attention on the contrary wisdom, which is the wisdom of loving relationship, the wisdom for which we were made, the wisdom which defines the limits of permissiveness.

ENDNOTES

Introduction: Mapping the Territory

1. Michel Foucault, *The History of Sexuality*, Vol. I (New York: Vintage Books, 1980), pp. 155-157.

2. See Helen Oppenheimer, *The Hope of Happiness* (London: S C M Press, 1983).

3. A full account of the single life must treat the question of homosexuality as indeed must any general treatment of the ethics of sex. The chapters of this volume do not address this subject directly and there is no specific chapter on it. This editorial decision was made for two reasons. The first is that the focus of this volume is on the relation between men and women and the second is that the issues involved in the debate over homosexuality are so complex that a single chapter cannot possibly do justice to them.

Chapter 1: Two Sexes

1. Phyllis Trible, *God and the Rhetoric of Sexuality* (Philadelphia: Fortress Press, 1978), p. 94.

2. See Mary Hayter, *The New Eve in Christ* (Grand Rapids: Eerdmans, 1987), pp. 16, 18, 40.

3. Melanie Klein differentiates anxiety and creativity in infant girls from those of infant boys. A girl tends (in unconscious fantasy) to fear attacks on the inside of her body, fears her insides will be scooped out, that she will be robbed, gutted. An infant boy fears attacks on the outside of his body, specifically that his genitals will be hurt or cut off, according to Klein. A girl experiences an inner creativity. She can draw things into herself and create

something out of her inner objects and fantasies. A boy knows the creativity of putting things out into the world of objects. Moreover, as discussed below, for Klein, persons of either sex experience both a feminine and a masculine position. In the feminine position our creativity takes the form of the urge to give life and to restore lost or injured objects. In the masculine position we experience fantasies of fertilizing and reviving injured internal objects. See Melanie Klein, *Envy & Gratitude & Other Works 1946-1963* (New York: Delacorte/Seymour Lawrence, 1975), chapters 6 and 8.

4. Vladimir Solovyev, *The Meaning of Love*, trans. Jane Marshall (London: Geoffrey Bles, 1945), p. 25.

5. See Karl Barth, *Church Dogmatics: A Selection* (Edinburgh: T. & T. Clark, 1961), pp. 194-204. I find myself in disagreement with Barth's typology of the sexes. It contradicts his own strong arguments against such rigid typologies.

6. See Nicholas Berdyaev, *The Meaning of the Creative Act*, trans. Donald A. Lowrie (New York: Collier, 1962), p. 168: "Sex is the source of being; the polarity of sex is the foundation of creation."

I cannot accept as convincing Berdyaev's argument that only the androgyne is the true likeness of God, because such an ascription of sexuality to God compromises the transcendence of the Holy. *We* are sexually differentiated, and our experience of sexuality, both between us and within us, gives us access to experiencing God. But the gap between creature and Creator is not crossed by projecting our sexuality into the divine.

7. For a discussion of "matriarchal" as opposed to the more familiar "patriarchal" superego, see Ann and Barry Ulanov, *Religion and the Unconscious* (Philadelphia: Westminster Press, 1975), pp. 145-55.

8. See Caroline Walker Bynum, *Jesus As Mother, Studies in the Spirituality of the High Middle Ages* (Berkeley: University of California Press, 1982); see also Elizabeth Petroff, *Consolations of the Blessed* (New York: Alta Gaia Society, 1979).

9. For further discussion of the feminine mode of consciousness and spirit, see Ann Belford Ulanov, *The Feminine in Jungian*

Psychology and in Christian Theology (Evanston: Northwestern University Press, 1971), chapter 9; see also Ann Belford Ulanov, *Receiving Woman: Studies in the Psychology and Theology of the Feminine* (Philadelphia: Westminster Press, 1981), chapter 3.

10. Paul Ricoeur, *Freud and Philosophy: An Essay on Interpretation*, trans. Denis Savage (New Haven: Yale University Press, 1970), p. 383: "Sexuality is not an isolated function alongside many others; it affects all behaviour. . . . Sexuality is a particular manner of living, a total engagement toward reality."

11. The spiritual urge toward union in sexuality makes dealing with sexuality in psychotherapy a volatile risk. See Ann Belford Ulanov, "Follow-Up Treatment in Cases of Patient-Therapist Sex," *Journal of American Academy of Psycho-Analysis* 7/1 (1979), pp. 101-110.

12. See Barry Ulanov, "The Limits of Permissiveness," in this volume.

13. See M. Masud R. Khan, "Pornography and the Politics of Rage and Subversion" in *Alienation in Perversions* (New York: International Universities Press, 1979), pp. 219-227. See also M. Masud R. Khan, "The Politics of Subversion and Rage" in *Times Literary Supplement*, February 4, 1972, pp. 121-122: "What masquerades as mutual and ecstatic intimacy through somatic events is in fact a sterile and alienated mental concoction."

14. A. R. Pope in "The Eros Aspect of the Eye" (Zurich: C. G. Jung Institute, Kleine Schriften, 1948) compares two kinds of seeing, both of which are involved in giving us "the eyes to see" what is there, as Scripture puts it. "Logos consciousness" of right-eye seeing looks into things to make something of them. "Eros seeing" of the left eye looks out, expressing the light of the unconscious.

15. See Ann Belford Ulanov, "The God You Touch" in *Christ and the Bodhisattva*, eds. Donald S. Lopez and Steven C. Rockefeller (Albany: State University of New York Press, 1987), pp. 118, 121-123.

16. See Melanie Klein, chapter 6.

17. See Alexander Lowen, *Depression and the Body: The Biologi-*

cal Basis of Faith and Reality (Baltimore: Penguin, 1972), p. 277.

18. See Melanie Klein, pp. 14, 41, 50, 58, 70, 73, 321.

19. See Barry Ulanov, *Prayers of St. Augustine* (Seabury, 1983).

20. See C. G. Jung, *Symbols of Transformation, Collected Works*, Vol. 5, trans. R.F.C. Hull (Princeton: Princeton University Press, Bollingen Series, xx, 1956), p. 437, para. 658. See also Ann and Barry Ulanov, *The Witch and the Clown: Two Archetypes of Human Sexuality* (Wilmette, Illinois: Chiron, 1987), pp. 225-230, 247-260, 271-278.

21. All examples are taken from my practice as psychoanalyst, with gratitude to those persons who allowed me to refer to their material.

22. C. G. Jung, *Mysterium Coniunctionis, Collected Works*, vol. 14, trans. R.F.C. Hull (New York: Pantheon, 1963), p. 183, para 670. See also *The Witch and the Clown*, pp. 73-86, 123-134, 135-160.

23. Sigmund Freud, "Femininity" in *New Introductory Lectures on Psychoanalysis*, trans. James Strachey (New York: Norton, 1964), pp. 112-117.

24. See Melanie Klein, chapters 6 and 8.

25. See D. W. Winnicott, *Playing and Reality* (London: Tavistock, 1971), chapter 5.

26. See D.W. Winnicott, "The Mother's Contribution to Society," in *Home Is Where We Start From*, ed. Clare Winnicott, Ray Shepherd, Madeleine Davis (New York: Norton, 1986), pp. 124-125; see also his "The Meaning of the Word 'Democracy'" in *ibid.*, pp. 252-253.

27. For a detailed discussion of the Fall as polarization, see Ulanov, *The Feminine*, pp. 296-303.

28. See *The Witch and the Clown*, pp. 140-151 for discussion of "Mute Acceptance."

29. For further discussion, see Ann Belford Ulanov, "Between Anxiety and Faith: The Role of the Feminine in Tillich's Theological Thought" in *Tillich on Creativity*, ed. Jacquelyn Kegley (Lanham, MD: University Press of America, 1988).

Chapter Two: Limited Engagements

1. See e.g., Susan Jacoby, "Risky Business," *The New York Times Magazine*, April 24, 1988: 26, 28.

2. See William Werpehowski, "The Pathos and Promise of Christian Ethics: A Study of the Abortion Debate," *Horizons* 12/2 (1985), p. 286.

3. *Ibid.*, 287.

4. See Philip Turner, *Sexual Ethics and the Attack on Traditional Morality* (Cincinnati: Forward Movement Publications, 1988). An earlier and very brief form of other parts of the argument which follows appears also in this booklet is the first of the Sweeny Lectures delivered at Christ Church, Grosse Pointe, Michigan in January of 1988. These lectures have been endowed in honor of endowed in honor of Dr. Donald and Mary Margaret Sweeny. I would like to express my gratitude for the support the Sweeny family provided me in the early stages of working out the basic lines of the argument that follows.

5. *Ibid.* See also Philip Turner, *Sex, Money and Power* (Cambridge, MA: Cowley Publications, 1985), pp. 30-31.

6. For Bellah's discussion of the distinction between a church and a "life style enclave" see *Habits of the Heart: Individualism and Commitment in American Life* (New York: Harper and Row, 1985).

7. I have placed the term "traditional teaching" within quotation marks in this initial use to indicate that the phrase is in fact a "term of art" used to bring together elements of belief and practice that are now found together but which have evolved slowly both in respect to their meaning, order of precedence and evalutation. The history of the Christian teaching about sex and marriage is by no means uniform. It manifests both change and diversity. It is not even uniform in its present state in that there is still an argument going on about the meaning of its elements and about how they ought to be related one to another. Thus, when I use the phrase "traditional teaching" I use it to refer to what I take to be at present the most dominant rendition of a long tradition. For a helpful summary of the history of Christian thought on sex and mar-

riage see D. S. Bailey, *The Man-Woman Relation in Christian Thought*, (London: Longmans, 1959).

8. For a more detailed treatment of the meaning of the metaphor of "one flesh" see *Sex, Money and Power*, pp. 45-70.

9. For a more detailed discussion of these points see *Sex, Money and Power*, pp. 45-70.

10. See especially Paul Ramsey, *Fabricated Man: The Ethics of Genetic Control*, (New Haven, CT: Yale University Press, 1970) and Oliver O'Donovan, *Begotten Not Made* (Oxford: Oxford University Press, 1984).

11. Roger Scruton, *Sexual Desire: A Moral Philosophy of the Erotic* (New York: Free Press, 1986). Those who know Scruton's work will notice that the following argument owes an enormous amount to him. I presented a shortened version of his argument in *Sexual Ethics and the Attack on Traditional Morality*. In the argument that follows, however, I have made what I believe to be significant changes in and additions to both his argument and the previously printed summary of my own.

12. Scruton, p. 33.

13. *Ibid.*

14. *Ibid.*, p. 230.

15. *Ibid.*, p. 231.

16. See "We should support vows for committed relationships outside marriage ceremony" by Denise G. Haines, *The Episcopalian*, March 1987, p. 8.

17. James Nelson, *Embodiment: An Approach to Sexuality and Christian Theology* (Minneapolis: Augsburg Publishing House, 1978), p. 158.

18. *Ibid.*

19. W. H. Auden, "For the Time Being: A Christmas Oratorio," in *Collected Poems*, ed. Edward Mendelson (New York: Random House, 1976), p. 271.

20. Mention of both social and ecclesial renewal raises the vexed question of the relation between the common life of the church and that of the larger society within which Christians live

and the church exists. The focus of this essay has been upon what Christians ought to say and do about sexual relations within their own community. The limitations of space have prevented my addressing directly the question of what a sexual ethic for Christians has to do with the sexual ethic of the society of which they are a part. Obviously I intend to say that Christians ought to consider their sexual behavior as part of the witness they make. They ought, in short, to understand that by ordering their sexual lives in a chaste manner they make known not only what they believe God intends for the sexual relations of all people but also the nature of the relationship that exists between Christ and the church. Nevertheless, in public arguments over the law and public policy in respect to sex it will prove necessary for Christians to recommend their views within the *public* arena in terms that are generally negotiable. They will, in short, have to employ arguments from reason like those constructed by Roger Scruton if they wish to recommend their views about law and public policy to people who do not share their religious beliefs. Simple appeals to revelation or biblical authority like those now being made by the religious right will not prove very convincing either to significant numbers of Christians or to the large number of people who do not count themselves among that number.

Chapter Three: Two Shall Become One
1. Hyde v. Hyde 1866.

This essay represents not so much new thinking about the meaning of marriage as an attempt to sort out and defend thinking developed over a number of years. So I have drawn here and there on my own earlier explanations of what I still believe, including *Incarnation and Immanence* (London: Hodders and Stoughton, 1973), *The Marriage Bond* (The Faith Press, 1976), "Marriage as Illustrating Some Christian Doctrines", Appendix 4 of *Marriage, Divorce and the Church* (The Root Report, 1971), and "Marriage" in The Westminster *Dictionary of Christian Ethics*, ed. James Childress and John Macquarrie (Philadelphia: Westminster, 1986).

I am aware that in maintaining within this discussion of marriage a particular version of Christian "personalism" and trying to guard against false emphasis and likely misunderstanding, I have taken for granted and left aside large questions, especially the importance of procreation and the defence of the underlying assumption that, whatever else we want to say about it, stable monogamy is good for human creatures.

2. See D. S. Bailey, *The Man-Woman Relation in Christian Thought* (London: Longmans, 1959). Compare John Macquarrie, *Three Issues in Ethics* (New York: Harper & Row, 1970), p. 64.

3. *St. John Chrysostom on Marriage and Family Life* (Crestwood, NY: St. Vladimir's Seminary Press, 1986), p. 43; p. 113.

4. See Bailey, pp. 266-7, note 5.

5. "Natural Law and Christian Ethics" in *Duty and Discernment,* ed. G. R. Dunstan (London: SCM Press, 1975), p.36.

6. *Karl Barth, Church Dogmatics* III, p. 290.

7. J. Burgoyne, R. Omrod, M. Richards, *Divorce Matters* (London: Penguin, 1987), p. 84.

8. G. R. Dunstan, "The Marriage Covenant," a Cambridge University Sermon published in *Theology* (May 1975), pp. 246-7.

9. Philip Turner, "The Marriage Canons of the Episcopal Church: I Scripture and Tradition", *Anglican Theological Review* LXV: 387.

10. Reprinted in *Sermons or Homilies Appointed to be Read in Churches* (London: Prayer Book and Homily Society, 1986), p. 348; p. 349.

11. *Marriage, Divorce and the Church,* pp. 148f., note 21.

12. In the Mothers' Union Report, *New Dimensions (London:* S.P.C.K. 1972), Appendix C, paragraph 17.

13. See John Macquarrie, "The Nature of the Marriage Bond" in *Theology* (May 1975), p. 233, and Eric Mascall, *The Importance of Being Human* (Oxford: Oxford University Press, 1959), p. 45.

14. *Divorce: A Christian Perspective* (Cincinnati:Forward Movement Publications, 1983), pp. 9-10.

15. See A. O. Rorty, "A Literary Postscript" in *The Identities of Persons,* ed. A. O. Rorty (Berkeley: University of California Press,

1976).

16. *New Dimensions,* note 23, appendix C, par. 17.

17. *Love and Play* (London: W. H. Allen, 1984), pp. 20, 28.

18. See R. S. Downie and E. Telfer, *Respect for Persons* (New York: Allen and Unwin, 1970) and Michael Tooley, *Abortion and Infanticide* (Oxford: Clarendon Press, 1983).

19. *Divorce,* note 26, p. 7.

20. *Sex, Money and Power* (Cambridge, MA: Cowley Publications, 1985), p. 37.

21. *Church Dogmatics* III.1.2; III.1.3; III.4.1.

22. Cf. John Macquarrie, *The Shape of Christology* (London: SCM Press, 1966), pp. 110-111.

23. *Church Dogmatics* III. 1. 2. p. 182; ibid, p. 185; III. 1. 3. p. 290.

24. Mary Hayter, *The New Eve in Christ* (London: SPCK, 1987), p. 91.

25. *Church Dogmatics* III. 1. 3, p. 319; III. 4. 1, p. 153.

26. *Ibid* III. 4. 1, p. 128.

27. *Ibid,* III. 1. 3, p. 324; III. 4. 1, p. 117; p. 125.

28. See *Marriage, Divorce, and the Church,* appendix 4, pp. 33-34 (note 1). Edward Schillebeeckx in volume 1 of *Marriage: Human Reality and Saving Mystery, trans. N. D. Smith* (New York: Sheed and Ward, 1965) uses the phrase "reciprocal illumination" (p. 63).

29. *Marriage, Divorce and the Church,* appendix 4, p. 33 (note 1).

30. This paragraph and the next come from *Incarnation and Immanence,* note 1, pp. 172-3. The introduction of the word "consent" into the 1969 English divorce law, and still more the so-called "divorce by post" procedure, obscure but do not obliterate this significant distinction. See Roderick Phillips, *Putting Asunder* (Cambridge: Cambridge University Press, 1988), note 21, par. 59.

31. Cf. Helen Oppenheimer, "Homosexuality and Relationship" in *Christian Action Journal* (Autumn 1979), p. 10.

32. *Incarnation and Immanence,* pp. 99-100 (note 1).

Chapter Five: Love, Marriage and Friendship

1. D. H. Lawrence, *Women in Love* (New York: Viking Press, 1950), p. 462.

2. Thomas Aquinas, III *Contra Gentes,* 124.

3. Gilbert Meilaender, *Friendship: A Study in Theological Ethics,* (Notre Dame and London: University of Notre Dame Press, 1981), pp. 1-2.

4. Adele M. Fiske, *Friends and Friendship in the Monastic Tradition* (Cuernavaca, Mexico): CIDOC Cuaderno No. 51, 1970), p 462.

5. Aristotle, *The Nichomachean Ethics,* VIII, 1155a.

6. Meilaender, *Friendship,* p. 13.

7. Aristotle, *Ethics,* VIII, 1155a.

8. Cicero, *De Amicitia* VI, 20.

9. *Ibid.,* XIII. 47.

10. Plutarch, "On Having Many Friends," 93:2.

11. *Ibid.,* 94.

12. Augustine, *Confessions* 11. 5.

13. *Ibid.,* IV. 12.

14. Roger Scruton, *Sexual Desire: A Moral Philosophy of the Erotic,* (New York, Free Press, 1986), p. 89.

15. *Ibid.,* p. 244.

16. *Ibid.,* p. 232.

17. Thomas Aquinas, IV *Disputations IX de Potentia,* 9.

Chapter Six: The Limits of Permissiveness

1. See Fyodor Dostoevsky, *The Brothers Karamazov,* trans. Constance Garnett (New York: Modern Library, 1950), pp. 78-79. Ivan's argument is summarized by another character, Miusov.

2. See the opening pages of Philip Turner's "Limited Engagements," in which the nature of present-day sexual activity and the accompanying moral discourse and debate, in and out of the churches, are characterized succinctly.

3. This is not to say that sexual issues are unknown in the

works of the ancients or their Medieval or Renaissance successors. There is in these works, however, no simple-minded taking of sides or soap-box proselytizing. Rather, the imagination—literary, philosophical, theological—defines the presentation of positions in works such as Plato's *Symposium,* Andreas Capellanus's *De Amore,* Dante's *Convivio,* or Castiglione's *Book of the Courtier.* The result is a more complex set of arguments, often with a handsomely ironic edge, but not necessarily a less winning one.

4. The phrase achieved the status of a holy ejaculation in the revolutionary liturgy after the publication of *Chto delat? (What is to be done?),* in 1863. Nikolai Chernishevsky's novel presents the rhapsodic dreams of a young socialist, with paradise made palpable in the form of a crystal palace where the socialist community dwells in bliss. It is also the title of Lenin's most substantial and hard-headed theoretical work, deliberately chosen both to echo and to transform the earlier volume.

5. *The Brothers Karamazov,* p. 291.

6. *Ibid.,* pp. 281, 283, 287.

7. *Ibid.,* pp. 292-311.

8. "The first movement of the will and of any appetitive power is love." Thomas Aquinas, *Summa theologica,* Ia, 20, 1. The movement of the will towards the good—however it understands the good—is inherent in our nature. Richard Hooker sets forth the doctrine in elegant Elizabethan prose in Book I, part viii of his *Of the Laws of Ecclesiastical Polity:* "as every thing naturally and necessarily doth desire the utmost good and greatest perfection of Nature hath made it capable, even so man. Our felicity therefore being the object and accomplishment of our desire, we cannot but wish and covet it." But the will must be guided by reason: "If Reason err, we fall into evil, and are so far deprived of the general perfection we seek." So simply stated, so complex in its working through in our lives.

9. Swift's poem is not often reprinted in selections from his work; it should be. It is to be found in *The Poems of Jonathan Swift,* ed. Harold Williams (Oxford: Oxford University Press, 1958), vol.

2, p. 526. *Chamber Music* is the title of Joyce's first volume of poems, published in 1907, a gathering of verses small in size, highly accessible in their lyric simplicity, and with a characteristic robustness, as the double meaning of the title suggests.

10. See *The Collected Poems of W. B. Yeats* (New York: Macmillan, 1951), pp. 254-255, 252.

11. Augustine's treatment of the mystery of freedom, evil, and original sin is extensive and detailed over many volumes. Particularly relevant to this essay are his short treatise on the nature of the good, *De natura boni*, and the first part of *De moribus ecclesiae catholicae*, on happiness (*De beatitudine*) and on the law of love (*Amoris lex*).

12. See *The Complete Poetry of John Donne*, ed. J. T. Shawcross (Garden City: Anchor Books, 1967), p. 344.

13. I have attempted to convey some sense of the range, majesty, and psychological power of such readings of the Song in a number of publications, most compendiously in "The Song of Songs: The Rhetoric of Love," in vol. 4 of *The Bridge: A Yearbook of Judaeo-Christian Studies* (New York: Pantheon, 1961), pp. 89-118. No works more insistently proclaim the indissoluble connection of the life of the spirit and the life of the senses than the ardent commentaries on the Song, from Origen to the present.

14. Bernardino de Laredo, "That the Cross is the door by which we enter into love," in *The Spirit of the Spanish Mystics*, ed. and trans. Kathleen Pond (New York: Kennedy, 1958), pp. 18-19.

15. John of the Cross everywhere supports our understanding of this movement of creature toward creator, in his poems and in his prose commentaries, with particular lucidity in his "redactions" of *The Spiritual Canticle*, where he makes clear that the senses are not rejected in the mystical life but rather refreshed and delighted.

16. Worst, perhaps, of the appeasements offered the tortured sexual imagination are the enticements of voyeurism, where all one's participation is vicarious and none of it really assuages. A brilliant, engrossing, and shrewdly moralized narrative of where voyeurism can lead is provided by Pierre Choderlos de Laclos in his 1782 *Les Liaisons dangereuses* (translated as *Dangerous Ac-*

quaintances) in which Mme. de Merteuil, leader of the book's demonic seductions, invariably performed for her by others, falls victim at the end to a smallpox so severe it loses her an eye. That is surely the most appropriate punishment for the grande dame of voyeuses. I am speaking here of the epistolary novel, not the rather silly play made from it. Roger Vadim's film version, on the other hand, does capture much of the novel's corrosive irony.

17. As the genre has heated up, so have the commentaries. Two of the coolest inspections of the new romance, each in its own way scholarly, critical, and instructive, are Helen Hazen's *Endless Rapture: Rape, Romance, and the Female Imagination* (New York: Scribner, 1983), and Carol Thurston's *The Romance Revolution: Erotic Novels for Women and the Quest for a New Sexual Identity* (Urbana: University of Illinois Press, 1987). Both offer hope that something better will come from the examination of this large industry of popular culture than the sort of irresponsible criticism Thurston addresses when she says: "The romance, it would seem, is damned if it does portray a world in which women are oppressed and damned if it does not." (p. 218)

18. The German theologian Helmut Thielicke says it clearly: "Love—and even, as we have said, erotic love—engages the whole person. It arises whole and undivided, not through the conflict of decision. In love, then, the will does not seek to assert itself against opposing forces (as in Kant's teaching on duty). It wills that which love impels it to love. It is an element in love, or better, an agent of it." See Thielicke's *Being Human. . . Becoming Human: An Essay in Christian Anthropology*, trans. G.W.Bromiley (Garden City: Doubleday, 1984), p. 222. Pornography, especially the literature and photography of the airbrush, is not interested in the whole person. The person, in fact, is only an unfortunate detail in the pornographic process, something to be relegated to a caption under a picture of a bulbous female or a craggy male, where we may be edified to learn that he or she "likes to read" in his or her "spare moments." I would not agree with Thielicke that "Nudity in art is sexless because it is without mystery" (*The Ethics of Sex* [Cambridge: James Clarke, 1978], p. 76), but if he is right, then pornography is sexless, especially the airbrush genre, be-

cause it is certainly without mystery.

19. Boethius, *Contra Eutychen et Nestorium,* III, i. See Boethius, *The Theological Tractates,* trans. H.F. Stewart and E.K. Rand in the Loeb Classical Library (London: Heinemann, 1926), p. 85.

20. As G.F. Woods argues in *A Defence of Theological Ethics,* (Cambridge: Cambridge University Press, 1966), our ethical standards do not come from some world of physical reality outside ourselves or from application of impersonal standards that lack the elements of mercy and forgiveness, as the impersonal must. "Our primary experience is of personal being. We have a closer acquaintance with being persons than with being anything else." But the difficulty remains: "we are still quite unable to think adequately of what we know ourselves to be" (p. 96).

21. "When woman is rescued in the tales of bewitchment, it is always because she has reached out from her captivity to her prince." See chapter III, "Bewitchment," in Ann and Barry Ulanov, *The Witch and the Clown: Two Archetypes of Human Sexuality* (Wilmette: Chiron, 1987), for some suggestions of the positive value of invoking the archetypal prince and princess in sexual relationships.

22. Perhaps the most easily accessible of the translations of this lovely thirteenth-century *chante-fable* is the Roger and Laura Loomis collection of *Medieval Romances* (New York: Modern Library, 1957). Its resemblance to Boethius's *Consolation of Philosophy* does not end with its alternation of verse and prose passages; it offers, like the *Consolation,* a sort of allegorized wisdom. The King in childbed and the Queen making war with baked apples, eggs, and fresh cheeses indicate with ironic amusement the effects of a world turned topsy-turvy. The inversion of sex roles is momentarily entertaining but it is too much against nature to be anything more, finally, than ludicrous. The tale presents our genetic experimenters with a good-natured way to contemplate the implications of their dislocations of human sexuality.

23. Rabelais makes much of the wisdom of the Deuteronomic provisions in chapter 6 of Book III of his *Gargantua and Pantagruel.* His figure of wisdom, Pantagruel, cites this "law of Moses" as intrinsic to a sound philosophy of marriage, a significant counter-step to the fruitless quest of Panurge, Rabelais's

figure of vice, as he seeks to arrange an alliance with a woman that will somehow guarantee him against being cuckolded.

24. Bernard Shaw was persuaded in 1903, when he had finished his Don Juan play, *Man and Superman,* that the male of the species was "no longer, like Don Juan, victor in the duel of sex. Whether he has ever really been may be doubted: at all events the enormous superiority of Woman's natural position in this matter is telling with greater and greater force." It is women, he assures us, who make the race: "if women were as fastidious as men, morally or physically, there would be an end of the race." Moliere, it seems to me, was more realistic about the Don Juan disease. His *Don Juan, or the Feast of the Statue,* is as Shaw says "not a play for amorists." Nor is it a comedy, as billed, but a bitter sexual excursion in which the essential impotence of Don Juan cannot be concealed, even in the multiple guises of his devout and carefully defended hypocrisy. See Epistle Dedicatory to *Man and Superman* in Bernard Shaw, *Complete Plays with Prefaces* (New York: Dodd, Mead, l963), vol. 3, pp. 492, 497, 491.

25. "Part-object" is, in psychoanalytic jargon, an object which is part of a person, a buttock, a breast, a penis. Charles Rycroft defines the kind of use I am making of the term here: "The distinction between whole and part object is sometimes used to make a . . . distinction . . . between recognizing an object as a person whose feelings and needs are as important as one's own and treating an object as existing solely to satisfy one's own needs." See Rycroft's *A Critical Dictionary of Psychoanalysis* (New York: Basic Books, 1968), p. 101. In sexual encounters that amount to no more than the meeting of part-objects, it is as if in contradistinction to being called "into the depths of our nature," we are being summoned into the shallows, with nothing of greater moral consequence involved than the fact that we have made some sort of choice.

26. "The giving and receiving of sexual pleasure bring deep solace to body and soul. Greeting and being greeted as a whole person can restore hope in the enterprise of being human." See Ann Belford Ulanov, "Two Sexes," in this volume.

27. Andre the Chaplain (Andreas Capellanus), who officiated at the court of Countess Marie de Champagne in the twelfth century,

teases the teasers in his definitions of "pure love" and "mixed love." The "pure," he explains, "consists in the contemplation of the mind and the affection of the heart; it goes as far as the kiss and the embrace and the modest contact with the nude lover, omitting the final solace, for that is not permitted to those who wish to love purely." Andreas's ironic disposition does not allow him to define "modest contact with the nude lover," but even without the "final solace," this is hardly what we should call "contemplation of the mind." "Mixed love," we learn, "gets its effect from every delight of the flesh and culminates in the final act of Venus." *Mixed*?! See Andreas Cappellanus, *The Art of Courtly Love,* trans. J. J. Parry (New York: Norton, 1969), p. 122.

28. Eberhard Jungel, *God as the Mystery of the World,* trans. D. L. Guder (Grand Rapids: Eerdmans, 1983) p. 174. This passage is part of a provocative discussion of "The certainty of faith as the deprivation of security," itself a crucial section of the central part of the book, "On the Possibility of Thinking God."

29. It is not far-fetched, I think, to understand this sexual knowing as part of what Lorraine Code calls our *Epistemic Responsibility* in the book so titled. It joins an epistemology of the body to what Code calls "intellectual virtue," which she defines as "a matter of orientation toward one's knowledge-seeking self. In other words, for the intellectually virtuous, self-knowledge is as important as, and indeed complementary to, knowledge of the world. To achieve it, one must, presumably, be good at introspection, and this capacity, like the other qualities mentioned, can be cultivated in oneself, even though there are crucial conscious and unconscious limitations upon the extent to which self-knowledge can be achieved and/or claimed, even through introspection." See *Epistemic Responsibility* (Hanover, NH: University Press of New England, 1987), p. 57.

INDEX

A

Aelred of Rievaulx 163 - 164
Aquinas, Thomas 119, 128, 132 - 141, 143 - 145, 148, 176, 183
archetype 31 - 33, 145
Aristotle 125, 133, 137, 151 - 155, 157, 159, 161 - 162, 166 - 167, 169 - 170, 172
Auden, W. H. 75
Augustine 30, 151, 162 - 166, 187

B

Barth, Karl 5, 22, 90, 108 - 110, 166
Basil the Great 161
Body of Christ 126, 162, 164
Boethius 195

C

character 12, 17, 27, 51, 74, 109, 113, 120, 139 - 141, 143 - 145, 153, 155, 157 - 158, 167, 172, 200
charity 57, 59, 84, 124, 128, 134, 143, 146, 159, 163, 175
chastity 68, 74 - 75, 84 - 85, 87, 119
children 10, 28 - 29, 49 - 50, 56 - 58, 60, 88, 93, 103, 118 - 119, 121, 128, 139, 142, 164 - 165, 172, 174, 180, 197 - 198, 205
Chrysostom, John 89
Cicero 151 - 152, 155 - 156, 158 - 159, 162 - 163, 166, 170
commitment 73 - 75, 97, 99, 102, 121, 123, 156
community 1, 5, 7, 64, 67, 81 - 83, 96, 119 - 120, 139 - 141, 143 - 144, 146, 154, 159 - 162, 164, 173, 175, 198 - 199
contemplation 26, 30, 36, 194
covenant 60, 90 - 92, 96, 113
creation 19 - 20, 29 - 30, 39, 41, 56, 89 - 90, 100, 106, 109 - 110, 125, 129, 131, 134 - 135, 142
cross, the 17, 79, 84, 130, 189

D

depth psychology 29 - 31
desire 22, 25, 46, 51, 57, 59, 61 - 73, 75, 78, 83, 116 - 118, 121, 154, 166, 172 - 173, 175, 187 - 188, 206
divorce 54, 88, 91 - 93, 96, 103, 121, 173
Donne, John 187 - 189